Praise for the Grandparent Legacy Edition

My husband, Steve, and I –along with his siblings and spouses— have been praying for years for our extended family's grandchildren. Each week we pray for 60 grandkids and their parents by name. But THIS! *The Grandparent Legacy Edition of the Pray for Me Prayer Guide* will revolutionize how we pray for these children who are so dear to us. Now we will have a system, a Biblical plan and prayers aimed at a continuing spiritual influence long into their adult lives. Did I mention I love this? Well, I do! What grandparent wouldn't? Pick up this amazing tool that helps one generation to pray deeply and Biblically for another and then get ready to hit your knees!

Valerie Bell

Co-author *RESILIENT: Child Discipleship and the Fearless Future of the Church (2020)*
CEO/ Awana Clubs International
"Lovie" (my grandma name) to Rowan, Rhys, Merrick, Griffin, Elise and Dean

"Father God, thank you for the wisdom and guidance you have given to Tony Souder to develop this outstanding, multigenerational, prayer guide for churches. It is my fervent prayer and hope that You will indeed strengthen the faith and unity of Your Church as Your Word is prayed and proclaimed with urgency and clarity. May Your glory be magnified! Amen!"

Mrs. Tina Bradford

Legacy Coalition's Prayer Leader

I love praying for my grandchildren. Tony Souder has given me and so many more, a valuable tool to pray with intentionality and biblical focus. I will be a better man of prayer for my grandchildren by using this great resource.
Dave Butts

President, Harvest Prayer Ministries
Chairman, America's National Prayer Committee

Having been a Youth Pastor and Senior Pastor, and a Grandparent (Papa) for over a decade, I heartily recommend the Pray for Me Campaign, and Tony's Prayer Guide. There is no greater gift we can give our grandkids than our ongoing commitment to grow in our love for Jesus, and a commitment to bring them faithfully to the occupied throne of grace. Tony gives us clear, creative, flexible, paths to pray the Gospel deep into the hearts of our grandkids. Grateful for my brother and this ministry.
Scotty Smith

Pastor Emeritus, Christ Community Church, Franklin, TN; Teacher in Residence, West End Community Church, Nashville, TN, Author, Everyday Prayers

I'm delighted by Tony Souder's pioneering work to connect praying grandparents with their grandkids. There is nothing more powerful, more simple than a grandparent committing themselves to pray daily for their grandchildren. I pray daily for 14! Thank you Tony!
Paul E. Miller

Author of A Praying Life and J-Curve: Dying and Rising with Jesus in Everyday Life

There is no greater legacy than passing on faith from generation to generation. I don't believe there is anything more important for a Grandparent, than praying for and impacting their grandchildren. *Pray for Me* reminds us of our legacy and then gives us helpful tools to focus on this wonderful commitment. And to brag about Tony Souder for a moment...Tony is the real deal. Not only does he write with authority, he lives with integrity and faith. Please do not pass up this opportunity to influence your next generations for eternity.

Jim Burns, PhD

President, HomeWord

Author of *Doing Life With Your Adult Children: Keep Your Mouth Shut and the Welcome Mat Out*

In the *Grandparent Legacy Edition* of the *Pray for Me Prayer Guide*, my friend Tony Souder equips grandparents with a powerful plan for praying specifically for their grandchildren. For the grandparents who are looking to maximize, freshen, or deepen how they pray for their grandchildren, this book is the answer! The structure is extremely helpful, the focus is biblical, the plan is doable and the results will be wonderful! Of books that are available to grandparents to guide their prayers for their grands, this is one of the very most strategic and practical! Tony Souder and his book have my highest recommendation!

Larry Fowler

Founder, Legacy Coalition

As grandparents of 14 grandchildren and having spent five decades equipping youth leaders to reach and disciple the younger generation to follow Jesus, I am delighted to see what Tony—my longtime friend--has written to help us personally, and all believing grandparents in our praying. For us, most of our grandkids live long distances away. That distance has intensified our desire to pray for them. Because relationships are harder to build at a distance, prayer is our tool for being a transforming influence in our grandkids' lives. And because of our desire and great need, my enthusiasm level is very high for Tony's new book to help us express our prayers with more focus. The value of Tony's new book was brought home to me with this powerful quote from Ron Dunn: "Prayer is like a missile. It can fly at the speed of thought. It can reach any target anywhere, and there is no anti-ballistic missile that can shoot it down." My prayer is that the Lord will use this book to increase our prayer arsenal for our grandkids!

Barry St. Clair

Founder, Reach Out Youth Solutions

Pray for Me

GRANDPARENT LEGACY EDITION

Tony Souder

Copyright © 2021 by Tony Souder.

All rights reserved. No part of this publication may be reproduced, distributed or transmitted in any form or by any means, including photocopying, recording, or other electronic or mechanical methods, without the prior written permission of the publisher, except in the case of brief quotations embodied in critical reviews and certain other noncommercial uses permitted by copyright law. For permission requests, write to the publisher, addressed "Attention: Permissions Coordinator," at the address below.

Tony Souder/LeaderTreks
25W560 Geneva Road, Suite 30
Carol Stream, IL 60188
PrayforMeCampaign.com

Scripture quotations are from The Holy Bible, English Standard Version® (ESV®) Copyright © 2001 by Crossway, a publishing ministry of Good News Publishers. Used by permission.
All rights reserved.
ESV Text Edition: 2011

Cover Design by Cristina Smith

Pray for Me: Grandparent Legacy Edition/ Tony Souder. —1st ed.
ISBN 978-0-9963750-8-5

Contents

Acknowledgements

Preface

The Call

Introduction- Leaving a Legacy

Part One: The Adventure of Prayer

The Adventure of Prayer 21

Praying the Scriptures 23

The 7 Essentials 25

The See, Savor, Share Discipleship Process 41

Part Two: Five Weeks of the Seven Essentials

Five Weeks of Seven Essentials in Seven Days 49

Part Three: A Week of Each Essential

Week Six: Favor 96

Week Seven: Wisdom 105

Week Eight: Love 114

Week Nine: Faith 123

Week Ten: Purity 132

Week Eleven: Speech 141

Week Twelve: Conduct 150

Part Four:

Giving Blessings 161

Autumn Gold 175

Part Five: Additional Ways to Pray Scripture

Praying for their Salvation 203

Week Thirteen: Praying the Proverbs 213

Week Fourteen: Leverage Prayers 222

Appendix

Grandparent Survey Summary 231

Pete Austin III Prayer Approach 233

Pray for Me Campaign 239

Become a Movement Champion 240

Additional Resources 242

*This book is dedicated to Pete Austin IV (Pops)
and Bob Holt Sr. (Bobby)*

Long before you were ever smitten grandfathers, you were generationally minded visionary leaders who used your time, talent and treasure to bring the greatness of God to each emerging generation. Together you have provided a combined total of over forty-five years of wise, humble, resilient, faithful and visionary board leadership to the ministry of One Hundred Years. The impact of your lives on me personally and the ministry is incalculable.

May you and your families know the fullness of joy and peace in trusting and treasuring Christ for generations to come.

OUR PRAYER FOR EACH EMERGING GENERATION OF GRANDPARENTS:
May your resilience in praying for your grandchildren be an instrument in the hand of God for countless future generations to treasure Christ for all he is worth!

Acknowledgements

I am continually amazed at the impact of a simple question. This book is the result of one of those questions asked numerous times by a variety of people. The question was phrased like this: "Have you ever considered writing a grandparent edition of the Prayer Guide?" Usually they would follow their question with a series of statements in order to fortify their case concerning the importance of this particular edition of the Prayer Guide. I am thankful for their persistent persuasion. I want to specifically thank the five people who were the most persistent and persuasive in their promotion of the idea. In alphabetical order, they are: Deborah Addington, regional leader with Ignite 3:16 Children's ministry; Brian Crowe, retired Awana ministry veteran; Jane Ann Larsen, Director of Connections with Legacy Coalition; Walt Mueller, President of the Center for Parent Youth Understanding; and Dann Spader, Founder of Sonlife ministries. There were others who echoed the importance of equipping grandparents in praying for their grandchildren, but these were the instrumental few that God used to persuasively prompt me to pursue this project. Thank You!

As most things in life that matter, this project took the skills and talents of a whole host of people that are extremely important to me. Specifically I am thankful for our in-house *One Hundred Years* team: Mary Elizabeth Haynes Burton, Cristina Smith, Sylvia Carpenter, and Zach Wyatt. Thank you for your love for Jesus and commitment to excellence in helping every generation reach the next generation with the greatness of God.

One of my greatest joys with this project has been the privilege of interviewing grandparents from around the country. Their wells of wisdom are deep and their insights are compelling and clear. It was both an honor and deeply humbling to hear their stories. Their hopes, dreams, joys and challenges have shaped me and thus have helped shape this book. Thank you!

To my bride of over 35 years and counting, I am beyond grateful. Rhonda makes all things better. She has helped me become more than I ever thought I could be. One of her super powers is the ability to see people like Jesus sees them and treat them accordingly. I am the happy recipient of her super powers daily!

My daughters, Abby and Bethany, must be mentioned. Their joy and delight in Jesus and in me as their dad is a powerful reminder of how generational blessings can go both ways. Their constant encouragement inspires me to press on in all that God has called me to.

May God in his mercy use the collective goodness of all those who invested in this project to bless countless grandparents and grandchildren for generations to come.

Preface

Four decades ago when I was in the early stages of my youth ministry experience, I had no understanding of what the landscape of youth ministry would become. Who would have imagined that 50% of young people from good families and churches would be exiting the church and abandoning their faith after high school? Some would actually say that those statistics are conservative numbers.

A national report commissioned by the Pinetops Foundation, called The Great Opportunity, says:

- Over 35 million young people who were raised in Christian homes could walk away from a life with Jesus by 2050. (The Great Opportunity: 2018)

This is heartbreaking! These are young people in our midst, in our churches. They are regularly walking by us in our halls and sanctuaries. These young people are someone's grandchildren, maybe even one or more of yours. Unfortunately, if trends continue, these young people may soon be walking away from all of the love and hope that is promised in Christ. *It doesn't have to be this way, and I believe you and I can help!*

Did you know that every major study concerning the faith of young people over the last 20 years points to the indispensable role of adults in helping them flourish in their faith? Let that soak in! Every one of your grandchildren needs multiple believing adults like you and me who are investing in their lives if they are going to trust and treasure Christ for a lifetime. Forging these relationships must become one of our non-negotiable aims as the church. It is imperative, in order to help your grandchildren and every young person stay connected to the church and flourish in their faith for a lifetime.

Wayne Rice, who is a 50-year veteran of youth and family ministry, Co-Founder of Youth Specialties and author of "Long Distance Grandparenting", makes this profound statement.

> "Behind parents, grandparents are the most influential people in the lives of children and youth."
> Wayne Rice

I believe Wayne is right! I also believe that your prayers for and with your grandchildren can play a powerful role in how they flourish in faith and life. Godly grandparents can be game changers for their grandchildren! God, in his goodness and mercy, has given Christian grandparents a unique and powerful love and motivation to bless their grandchildren.

It is my desire that God will use the book you are holding to encourage and equip you to have a laser-like prayer focus as you seek to champion the cause of your grandchildren before the throne of God. When you pray for your grandchildren, you are forging a supernatural relational connection with them that is rooted in the character and purposes of God. This connection can become a stabilizing factor for their faith and life, as they grow older.

Linking the Generations through Prayer

Just in case you didn't know, this book is part of a larger movement called the Pray for Me Campaign that was started in January of 2014. The Pray for Me Campaign was specifically created to address the problem of young people leaving the church and abandoning their faith in early adulthood. Of course there are complex reasons behind the large numbers of young people abandoning the church and their faith. However, research has shown that those young people who stay connected to the church and flourish in their faith tend to be marked by having multiple adult believers investing in their lives. Don't miss the magnitude of that sentence. Intergenerational relationships matter for lasting faith. Creating multiple Christ-centered intergenerational relationships are essential in helping young people stay connected to the church and flourish in faith and life for a lifetime.

> The Pray for Me Campaign is the result of asking a simple, yet strategic question: How can we help more adults connect with more young people more naturally than ever before?

That question has started a movement: a movement to help every young person connected to the church have the relationships they need to flourish in faith and life beginning with prayer. Through the Pray for Me Campaign young people are equipped to invite three adults from different generations to pray for them for a year. Each year these young people invite three new adults to pray, giving them a growing and robust web of adult relationships rooted in prayer.

The movement is growing: In the years since its inception, God has used the Pray for Me Campaign to help over 600 churches in 42 states create over 50,000 intergenerational relationships rooted in prayer. (For more information about the Pray for Me Campaign, see appendix.)

Every child in every church is someone's grandchild.

Our vision is that every grandchild would have a vast web of caring adults who are willing to champion their cause before the throne of God. I believe the 30 million Christian grandparents in the United States can play a significant role in whether or not the emerging generations will trust and treasure Christ for a lifetime. What if the grandparents in every church, not only became Prayer Champions for their own grandchildren, but also became a catalyst for launching the Pray for Me Campaign in their church? This one action would mean that every grandchild in each of these churches would have the Christ-centered relationships they need to flourish in faith and life for a lifetime. These simple and yet profound efforts could impact generations to come.

Thank you for your role in this "Grand" endeavor!

The Call

Just imagine if the concern on the minds of members of the older generation was not, "I just don't know why I am still here." What if the refrain; "I am just a dinosaur, old, outdated, unimportant and forgotten!" was never heard again? How glorious might it be if these melancholy repetitions were replaced with "I am a watchman on the wall of God's City! I take my place with warrior-like vigilance to cry out for those who now fill the living rooms of the families I love, the school rooms of the academies that serve the youth of this city and the community within which I live. I live my life now to fight in prayer for the spiritual life of the next generation. Those younger than me will not live their lives, will not struggle in this fallen world without my vigilant prayer cover. I am living for their well-being. I am praying for their flourishing! That is why I am here! I am a watchman on the wall!"

Tony Souder has called you, grandfather and grandmother, to not step down but kneel down; to not step back but step up! He is asking you to just imagine! What would happen if the homes where grandchildren love to visit, assisted living facilities and nursing homes of our society became "houses of prayer?" What if those of us with more of God's time spent more of that time interceding for our grandchildren than bemoaning our grandkids' spiritual condition?

This is strong medicine for us grandparents. Oh, how we need this! Heed the call! Join and become a watchman on the wall!

Joe Novenson, Pastor of Senior Adults, Lookout Mountain Presbyterian Church

Before God enables his people to bring in a harvest, he pours out a Spirit of prayer upon them. The surest sign that God is about to send power upon us is a great movement of prayer in our midst.

—JOHN PIPER

INTRODUCTION

Leaving a Legacy

A PREMATURE OBITUARY! What if tomorrow you were perusing the obituaries and found yours? That's what happened to Alfred Nobel in April of 1888 while reading a newspaper in Paris. A newspaper mistakenly reported Alfred's demise when it was actually his brother Ludvig who died of a heart attack. The title that was given for Alfred's premature obit was "The Merchant of Death is Dead". That sounds like an ominous oxymoron since most of us know Alfred Nobel as the founder of the Nobel Peace Prize. Alfred was a scientist and inventor whose most famous and lucrative invention was dynamite, which was used in both construction and warfare. Some historians see this newspaper's faux pas as one of several things that led Alfred to ultimately dedicate the majority of his vast fortune, $265 million in today's funds, to establishing the Nobel Peace Prize. To whatever extent the premature obituary influenced Nobel's life, there is no doubt that he ultimately took some decisive steps to change the ending of his story from merchant of death to promoter of peace.

So what about you? How would your premature obituary read? Since no one is likely to make the mistake of writing your obituary before your actual demise, how would your obit read today and how would you want to change the ending? I realize those are weighty questions and definitely worthy of some extended thought. However, my main interest concerns your spiritual legacy and how this Grandparent Legacy Edition Prayer Guide can serve to help you flourish in leaving a lasting spiritual legacy.

Prayer: The Path to a Spiritual Legacy

There are a lot of things that impact the strength of our spiritual legacy. However, at the core of any spiritual legacy is our own personal relationship with God. Ultimately, it is how we personally walk with God, that fuels what our spiritual legacy will actually become and prayer is vital in this process. Yes, vital! Prayer is actually what makes our relationship with God a *real* relationship. Prayer plays a unique and powerful role in how we relate with the God of the universe. Let me explain: God has mercifully made himself clearly and powerfully known through the means of Creation, His Word, the person of Jesus and the Holy Spirit. And yet, it is in the gift of Prayer that God has made it possible for us to respond and interact with Him concerning all that he has revealed about himself and our world. Remember, prayer makes our relationship with God a *real relationship*. Here's the negative way to say it: WITHOUT PRAYER THERE IS NO RELATIONSHIP WITH GOD.

Over the years I have become more and more convinced that our relationship with God in prayer is magnificently multifaceted. Here are three facets of what I mean. First, when we pray, God changes us. He uses our time with him in prayer to soften our hearts, draw us ever closer to himself and conform us into the image of his son. Secondly, God uses our prayers to carry out his purposes, impacting people and situations around the world for his glory and their good. That is simply astonishing. The third aspect is the supernatural connecting power of prayer. God uses our prayers for others to supernaturally connect us in ways far beyond what we could imagine, both to him and those for whom we are praying. Each of these facets of prayer influences your spiritual legacy. The importance and impact of your prayers for your grandchildren is incalculable.

Layers of Goodness

This Prayer Guide is not one-dimensional. There are layers of goodness in these pages waiting to be soaked in, so that lives can be transformed. The Prayer Guide is divided into five "Parts" that are designed to strengthen your understanding and engagement in prayer for your grandchildren and others. All five parts of the Prayer Guide are very important—each for a different reason.

PART ONE: This part is extremely important because it lays out the core components of how the daily prayers are structured. It highlights the fresh adventure of prayer, along with the power of praying scripture based prayers. It reveals the value of praying through the lens of the 7 Essentials as well as the sweetness of the See, Savor and Share discipleship process. This section provides you with the "AHA's" of understanding you will need to fully enjoy the rest of the Prayer Guide.

PART TWO: With the understanding of "Part One" firmly in hand, Part Two launches into five weeks of praying the 7 Essentials in 7 days. This part provides you with a balanced way of praying each of the 7 Essentials for your grandchildren.

PART THREE: Provides you with the opportunity to pray each of the 7 Essentials in a more extended way. It will be like doing a one-week deep dive into each of the 7 Essentials by focusing on praying through the lens of one Essential for an entire week.

PART FOUR: This part is one of my favorites because it unveils the beauty and bonding power of giving your grandchildren blessings. As you will see, giving blessings to your grandchildren can be a transformative experience. This section also provides the "Autumn Gold Gleanings", which is a summary of the grandparent interviews that I conducted.

PART FIVE: This section provides a trifecta of prayer goodness by focusing on praying for your grandchildren's salvation, Praying the Proverbs, and praying what I call "Leverage Prayers".

Using this Prayer Guide will help you flourish in being a Prayer Champion for your grandchildren. You may not feel like a Prayer Champion and I totally understand that feeling. However, when I talk about you being a Prayer Champion I don't mean you are the best "pray-er" around. I simply mean you are someone willing to champion the cause of your grandchildren before the throne of God. This book will guide you in pursuing God's provision, protection, and purposes in the lives of all those you pray for; and when we intentionally pray for others, something amazing happens inside of us as well. The capacity of our hearts to love and enjoy God and others begins to expand. We begin to move toward others to bless and encourage them in ways beyond prayer. This book is designed with that in mind.

Jesus, The Golden Rule and Intentional Prayer

How many times have you been asked to pray for someone only to forget about it later on? You are not alone. Fortunately, my attentiveness to prayer was transformed one day when I was sitting in a hospital room after my wife's surgery in Long Island, New York. It wasn't like I was looking for transformation that day; I was minding my own business, reading through the Gospel of Matthew, when God opened my eyes to see a truth that in my blindness I had overlooked every other time I had read the familiar passage found in Matthew 7:7-12.

> *Ask and it will be given to you; seek, and you will find; knock, and it will be opened to you. For everyone who asks receives, and the one who seeks finds, and to the one who knocks it will be opened. Or which one of you, if his son asks him for bread, will give him a stone? Or if he asks for a fish, will give him a serpent? If you then, who are evil, know how to give good gifts to your children, how much more will your Father who is in heaven give good things to those who ask him!* (ESV)

If you were looking at your Bible you would know the above passage is not complete, it is only Matthew 7:7-11. We typically stop at verse 11, but Jesus doesn't stop his thought there. He goes on to a verse I am very confident that you know and yet, may be surprised to find here in this context. It is the Golden Rule: "So whatever you wish that others would do to you, do also to them, for this is the Law and the Prophets" (Matthew 7:12).

Jesus put The Golden Rule right at the culminating point of a passage about deliberate, persistent, hopeful prayer. So here is my takeaway from that hospital room years ago: Jesus wants you to approach prayer for your grandchildren and others with the same intensity and hopeful expectation as we would want them to approach praying for us. Here is the point: when we are in need, we don't want people to pray casually. We want them to pray with purposeful intensity because we know that in God's mercy and providence their prayers could change our situations. When I was in that hospital room I knew how I wanted people to be praying for my wife and me, and it wasn't casual prayer. I encourage you to let the Golden Rule shape the intensity and hopeful expectation of your prayers for your grandchildren and all that they are facing and will face as they grow up.

How do you want your grandchildren to eulogize you?

Let's finish where we started. Since we began with a premature obituary, it seems appropriate to conclude with a eulogy question. So here it is: How do you want your grandchildren to eulogize you? Truthfully, I love this kind of question. It helps me consider my hopes and desires for the future while at the same time making it personal for how I live today. As you ponder this question it's important to remember that a eulogy is different from an obituary. Obituaries typically are driven by the accomplishments and the highlights of a person's life. However, a eulogy has a more personal flavor.

Imagine with me for a moment the following scene: You have gone to meet Jesus face-to-face. All those you have known and loved along the way are gathered together for a celebration of life service, your funeral. A pastor guides the service and there are several people who stand and say cool things about you, they eulogize you. They share stories about the qualities of your character and how doing life with you made an impact on their lives. Then your grandchildren speak. What do they say about you? What aspects of your character do they remember and highlight? The great thing about reading and thinking about these questions now is that we still have time to influence their answers.

By God's grace working in and through us, we can take some decisive steps in our daily lives to purposefully influence the end of our stories. When we structure our lives to think, act and pray generationally we are setting the stage for a lasting spiritual legacy.

One of my favorite passages that inspires me to be intentional in thinking, acting and praying generationally is Psalm 71:17,18:

> *O God, from my youth you have taught me,*
> *and I still proclaim your wondrous deeds.*
> *So even to old age and gray hairs,*
> *O God, do not forsake me,*
> *until I proclaim your might to another generation,*
> *your power to all those to come. (ESV)*

The Psalmist remembers the goodness of God from his youth and longs to use the last season of his life to share with emerging generations what he has seen and savored concerning the greatness of God. He's my hero. I want to be like him.

So, what kind of spiritual legacy do you want to establish for your grandchildren and the generations to come? Let's start with prayer.

When Love Rescues the Lost

At 14 years old, Jessie was lost, carrying burdens too heavy for a teenager.

Through one of her prayer champions Lucy, Jessie first experienced God's love for her.

Lucy prayed all year for Jessie and the Holy Spirit surrounded Jessie with an older generation of believers who welcomed her doubts, related to her wrestling, and yet also pointed her to truth.

Ultimately, God faithfully answered Lucy's prayers for Jessie to seek truth and find freedom in following Jesus.

When Lucy and Jessie committed to the Pray For Me Campaign, prayer fostered a transforming relationship, bringing light into dark places, truth to doubts, and eventually salvation to one of God's children.

PART ONE

The Adventure of Prayer

Welcome to the adventure of praying for your grandchildren. Yes, it is an adventure! Life with God is always an adventure and prayer is at the very heart of it. The adventure of prayer is only accentuated by the deep love you have for your grandchildren. However, one of the primary pieces that makes prayer an adventure for me is that it is future focused. When we pray we are aiming into the future, whether it is the next second or the next decade. We are calling out to God, looking for him to show up with his sovereign goodness, mercy and power in some specific way to bring glory to his name and blessing to our world. As you pray scriptural prayers for your grandchildren, you are tapping into the economy of God. You are reaching into the future for God's glory and your grandchildren's good. Through your prayers you can provide layers of what I call time-released blessings on your grandchildren and great grandchildren. This is possible only because our prayers are rooted in God and all that he is. Our heavenly Father supersedes all time and oversees all eternity. He is able to answer your prayers for your grandchildren and great grandchildren aimed deep into the future, long after you have passed on to be face to face with King Jesus. Each of us can be an instrument of good in the hand of God for generations to come through our prayers. Now that is an adventure worth pursuing.

As in most adventures, the element of the unknown is always present. As you launch into praying, in perhaps a new way for your grandchildren, do not be surprised by how God draws you into an expanded and more robust prayer life as you take this journey. It is not unusual for those who are using the Pray for Me Prayer Guides to find themselves expanding the scope of who they pray for as they are praying for those they care for most. Of course everyone you pray for matters and the truth is that we *all* need people asking the King of the universe to bring his goodness to bear on our lives. One of my hopes is that prayer itself and the sharing of prayer needs between you and your grandchildren will become a natural and regular rhythm in your relationship. That each of you will find yourselves mutually praying for each other. Enjoy this journey.

Three Primary Components

As you move through this prayer guide you will experience the goodness of three primary components. They are brought together to provide a unique combination of goodness to help you flourish as you pray for your grandchildren. They are designed to give your prayers focus, clarity and consistency as they are woven throughout the prayer guide. These components are:
- Praying the Scriptures
- Praying through the 7 Essentials
- Utilizing the See, Savor, Share Discipleship Process

Praying the Scriptures

We begin by establishing our roots in the truths of Scripture. The Bible is the Word of God and as such has the power to give life to us and our prayers. Praying Scripture is one of the most powerful and authoritative ways to pray. Throughout this book you will experience the benefits of turning Scripture into prayers for your grandchildren. As we begin let's take a moment to be reminded of some of the promises that await us as we soak in the Scriptures.

The Word of God:

- Points us to Jesus (Luke 24:27)
- Strengthens (Psalm 119:28)
- Guards from sin and keeps us pure (Psalm 119:9, 11)
- Creates and sustains the universe (Psalm 33:6, 2 Peter 3:5, Hebrews 1:3, 11:3)
- Creates spiritual life (1 Peter 1:23, James 1:18)
- Is able to save our souls (James 1:21)
- Is living and active and able to discern the thoughts and intentions of the heart (Hebrews 4:12)
- Produces faith (Romans 10:17)
- Teaches, reproves, corrects, and trains in righteousness (2 Timothy 3:16)

These passages offer a small taste of all the goodness that flows from the supremacy and power of the Word of God.

One of the compelling aspects about the Pray for Me Prayer Guide is that it takes the most powerful words in the world, the very words of God, and makes them the catalyst for our prayers for your grandchildren and anyone else you are inclined to pray for.

The apostle Paul refers to the Scriptures as the Sword of the Spirit, and we know from Hebrews 4:12 that "the word of God is living and active, sharper than any two-edged sword, piercing to the division of soul and of spirit, of joints and of marrow, and discerning the thoughts and intentions of the heart." God uses his Word to transform our hearts whether it is written, spoken, or uttered silently in prayer to the Father. In this prayer guide I am committed to letting the very truths of Scripture be the kindling to set our prayers on fire with passion and purpose. Each day passages of Scripture that relate to the 7 Essentials have been turned into life-giving prayers for your grandchildren.

Praying like the Psalmist Prays

It would be hard to have a Scripture-centered prayer guide that didn't in some way point to the primary prayer and songbook in the Bible. Therefore, we will be taking cues from the Psalms in our efforts to turn Scriptures into prayers. They reveal a plethora of ways to plead with God. The beauty of the Psalms is that they portray the full spectrum of emotions and challenges that a human can experience. There is a grittiness and authenticity that we can relate to because it represents real life. Perusing the Psalms helps promote clarity, honesty, urgency, and directness in our prayers. Let's look at a few phrases from Psalm 119 that can give us a glimpse into the psalmist's directness and dependence on God in prayer:

- Do good to your servant (17)
- Open my eyes that I may see (18)
- Remove from me scorn... (22)
- Preserve my life according to your word (25)
- Teach me your decrees (26)

- Let me understand the teaching of your precepts (27)
- Strengthen me (28)
- Keep me from deceitful ways (29)
- Do not let me be put to shame (31)
- Give me… (34)
- Direct me… (35)
- Turn my heart… (36)
- Turn my eyes… (37)
- Fulfill your promise… (38)
- Take away… (39)
- May your unfailing love… (41)
- Do not snatch your word from my mouth (43)
- Remember… (49)
- Be gracious (58)
- Let your compassion… (77)

Each of these phrases is a clear call for God to act; a plea for the favor of God to act on the psalmists' behalf. As you turn Scripture into prayer for your grandchildren, you are ushering a clear call for God to act on their behalf. May God be ever so gracious to act and intervene for the good of each of your grandchildren for generations to come! May he cause you to be relentless in your prayers and your intentionality in bringing his greatness to them. May God soften their hearts to his greatness and grant them faithful responsiveness to his Word.

Praying Through The 7 Essentials

The second component of the prayer guide is structured around what I call The 7 Essentials. These seven biblical categories of life are the minimum essentials that I believe need to be attended to for someone to flourish in living faithfully before God and man.

The 7 Essentials come directly from two passages of the Bible, but their importance saturates all of Scripture. The first two, wisdom and favor, come from Luke 2:52: "And Jesus increased in **wisdom** and in stature and in **favor** with God and man." It is not surprising that Jesus grew in wisdom and favor because he was God in human form. What is surprising is that Luke makes sure that we know Jesus grew in wisdom and favor. Luke could have said anything he wanted about Jesus, but he made a point to let us know that wisdom and favor with God were essential, even for the Son of God. If it was essential for God's Son to grow in wisdom and favor, then there is no question that these two are essential for you and your grandchildren. The other five Essentials are found in 1 Timothy 4:12: "Let no one despise you for your youth, but set the believers an example in **speech**, in **conduct**, in **love**, in **faith**, in **purity**."

It is crucial to understand that Paul is not using throwaway words here. He is giving Timothy the essential categories that he needs to pay attention to in order to set an appropriate example for all believers. There was a lot at stake in this simple and precise directive from Paul to Timothy. These categories remain essential for us today.

So what does it mean to pray through the 7 Essentials for your grandchildren? Praying through the 7 Essentials simply means:

> Praying the TRUTHS of Scripture over the NEEDS of your grandchildren using the LENS of the 7 Essentials.

The breadth and scope of the 7 Essentials allows you to pray effectively for the full spectrum of needs that arise in your grandchildren's lives over time. One of your greatest needs is awareness. God forbid that anyone would be aloof and happily ignorant of what their grandchildren are facing. May God help you to be both curious and gentle concerning what is going on in their lives. This will fuel your ability to pray with precision and effectiveness.

In this prayer guide The 7 Essentials have been arranged into three categories based on the role of each Essential:

- The Favor Foundation: Favor
- The Core Four: Wisdom, Love, Faith, and Purity
- The Public Relations (PR) Pair: Speech and Conduct

The Favor Foundation

Foundations matter. In 2013 a 408-foot spire was lifted to the top of the new One World Trade Center in New York City making it the tallest building in the Western Hemisphere at 1,776 feet. Its stunning structure graces the Manhattan skyline. As we marvel at the grandeur of such a structure, how often do we take time to consider its foundation? Foundations are easily forgotten and yet they are indispensable. Oftentimes we forget that God's favor is the foundation of our lives. It is a strong and secure foundation, but in this world that values self-reliance, it is easy to forget that we are completely dependent on him. Think of God's favor as anything he does in, through, or for you. We can see the favor of God in his provision, protection, presence, and purposes.

The Essential of Favor

There is no aspect of our lives that is not touched by the favor of God. God's favor toward us is all encompassing. We get a glimpse of this in the following passages.

> **Acts 17:28** *"In him we live and move and have our being."*
> **Romans 11:36** *"For from him and through him and to him are all things."*
> **Colossians 1:15-17** *"He [Jesus] is the image of the invisible God, the firstborn of creation. For by him all things were created, in heaven and on earth, visible and invisible, whether thrones or dominions or rulers or authorities—all things were created through him and for him. And he is before all things,* **and in him all things hold together.***" (Emphasis added)*

It's worth stating again, there is no aspect of our lives that is not touched by God's all-encompassing creating and sustaining favor.

Here is a taste of some of what God's favor includes:
- The beating of our hearts.
- The breath in our lungs.
- It fuels the giggling joy of a small grandchild being tossed in the air by her loving grandfather.

But, God's favor is also:
- Conviction of sin, forgiveness, repentance and faith.
- It is love, joy, peace, patience and the rest of the fruit of the Spirit.

Our entire existence flows from God's creating and sustaining favor.

I want to encourage you to become a "Favor Collector". A Favor collector is someone who seeks to identify and treasure the whole gamut of God's favor in our lives, the big and small things, along with the seen and unseen. This is not something we can do on our own. We actually need the favor of God in order to see the favor of God in our lives. God in his mercy provides what we need; he gives us both the Holy Spirit and His Word to help us understand the scope of his favor. Our job is to seek to be in tune with the Spirit and the Word. We need to take our cue from the Psalmist who prays so directly as we saw a few pages back, "Open my eyes that I may behold wondrous things from your law" (Ps.119:18); "Incline my heart to your testimonies" (Ps. 119:36) and the list goes on.

Our need for the Favor of God to see the Favor of God is why one of my favorite prayers for myself and others is:

"Father, in your mercy give us eyes to see, ears to hear, and humble hearts to understand and embrace your favor in all of life."

Take a moment right now. Pull out a journal or a digital device and begin listing some of the ways you are seeing the Favor of God in your life and your grandchildren's lives. If you are having trouble thinking of things, consider making the above prayer a part of your daily rhythm. As you do this, remember it isn't a race; our heavenly Father will answer. He delights to help his children see, hear and understand his favor and goodness around them. Take some time to hover over what you are seeing. Let the goodness you are seeing soak into your soul. This will be fuel for the See, Savor, Share process that we will look at in the coming pages.

Favor, God's favor, is the foundation for all the other Essentials. As you pray for God's favor in your grandchildren's lives here are a couple of things to keep in mind. First, your prayers don't have to be perfect. God knows what they need and when you generally pray his favor over their lives he can meet their needs with his wisdom and power according to his perfect timing. Second, when you become aware of specific areas of need don't hesitate to ask God to lavish his specific favor over their specific needs. To help make praying God's favor over specific needs a little easier, I have outlined a practical four step process below. Enjoy!

A Four Step Process

Here is a 4 step process that is helpful when you are trying to pray specific favor over specific needs for your grandchildren.

Step One: Identify a need: Anxiety

The truth is that each of us have specific places where we need extra doses of God's favor.

Step Two: Determine what aspect of the Favor of God addresses the need of anxiety.

Of course there are multiple ways to pray for God's favor concerning anxiety depending on its specific cause. However, a simple way to determine the direction of your prayers is to ask this question: What is the opposite of being anxious? Answer: Peacefulness. The peace of God can satisfy the anxious heart.

Step Three: Find a scripture passage or truth from the Bible that speaks to the aspect of God's favor that you identified in step two.

2 Thessalonians 3:16 "Now may the Lord of Peace himself give you peace at all times and in every way."

Step Four: Turn that passage into a prayer.

A Prayer for Favor

Father, you are the Lord of Peace and we pray that you would help us to know your peace and presence at all times and in every way. Cause your favor to rest on us today. Help us to surrender all of our anxiety and fear to you, that we may know your peace that surpasses all understanding. Strengthen us to be your people of peace, so that our lives would point our friends, neighbors and communities to you. We pray this for your glory and our good, in the name of the Prince of Peace, Jesus, amen.

The Core Four

I call wisdom, love, faith, and purity the Core Four because they reflect the condition of our hearts. They represent the substance of who we are. It is in these areas that we need God to unleash his favor first and foremost. So let's take some time and dive into each of these Essentials which will set the stage for you as you seek to pray for your grandchildren through these lenses.

The Essential of Wisdom

It cannot be overstated how important wisdom is for all of our lives, including your grandchildren. Every day we experience the blessings and benefits of other people's wise choices. We don't think about them, we just enjoy them. Sometimes we actually may even take them for granted.

Unfortunately, the value of wisdom too often shines the brightest when it is seen in contrast to foolishness. All of us have felt the pain of foolishness, either from our own foolish decisions or from someone else's. Your grandchildren are making decisions every day that will affect the rest of their lives. It is heartbreaking to see so many young people continually making foolish decisions that wreak havoc on their own lives and the lives of those around them.

As Christian grandparents it is your desire that God would use your prayers to enhance your "grands'" wisdom so they can make better decisions—and to reduce their regrets from poor, unwise decisions. To help move in this direction, here are 3 of my favorite ways of praying over each emerging generation.

1. <u>Pray that they will WANT Wisdom.</u> They will not pursue what they do not want. It's the same for each of us. Pray that the taste buds of their hearts and minds would crave the sweetness of wisdom and savor it daily.

2. <u>Pray that they would have eyes to SEE Jesus for all he is worth!</u> Colossians 2:3 says that "in whom [Jesus] are hidden all the treasures of wisdom and knowledge". As you pray for your grandchildren's relationship with Jesus to deepen, you are also addressing their need for greater and greater wisdom. They will begin to understand life more clearly as Jesus becomes clearer to them.

3. <u>Pray they will walk with the wise.</u> Proverbs 13:20 says, "He who walks with the wise becomes wise, but the companion of fools will suffer harm." Oh that each of your grandchildren would have a propensity for people who are wise.

A Prayer for Wisdom:

Father, all of life and wisdom come from you. Cause each of us to be relentless in our desire and pursuit of your wisdom. Thank you for packaging all of your treasures of wisdom and knowledge in the person of Jesus. Help us to see and savor him for all he is worth. In your mercy and kindness give each of us the wisdom to spot foolishness and flee it. Cause our hearts to align with those who love your ways and walk in your wisdom. We pray this for your glory and our good, in Jesus' name, Amen.

The Essential of Love

The apostle Paul prays a stunning prayer in Ephesians 3:14-21. He is praying that God would give us the strength to comprehend the incomprehensible. He prays for us to know the full spectrum of the love of Christ, its breadth, length, height and depth. He doesn't want us to miss any angle or dimension concerning the wonder of Christ's love. It is an amazing prayer. Scripture tells us that God is love, so it should not surprise us that Paul is putting so much emphasis on it in this passage. Of course, the greatest display of God's love is the Cross. Jesus, dying for our sins to bring us to God. Jesus goes so far as to say in Matthew 22:37-40 that our love for God and others is what the Law and the prophets is all about.

And he said to him, "You shall love the Lord your God with all your heart and with all your soul and with all your mind. This is the great and first commandment. And a second is like it: You shall love your neighbor as yourself. On these two commandments depend all the Law and the Prophets."

Here is a different question about love: Where in the Bible does God reveal his great delight for his children? There are many, but one of my favorite passages is Zephaniah 3:17. It goes like this:
"The Lord your God is in your midst, a mighty one who will save;
He will rejoice over you with gladness;
He will quiet you with his love;
He will exult over you with loud singing!"

Get a picture of that clearly in your mind. God's delight, pleasure, and enjoyment of his children cannot be contained. It explodes into a joyful song over his children.

I am stunned every time I hover over this passage. Here is one of my takeaways:

"God has an uncontainable exuberant delight in US as his children!"

Let that soak in. He is crazy about his children and your grandchildren need to know and feel this goodness deep in their souls.

A Prayer for Love

Father, you are great and glorious. Thank you for always being in our midst and for being our mighty savior. We rejoice that you rejoice over us with gladness. Thank you for calming our hearts with your love and for giving us a glimpse into how you sing and delight in your children. Cause our songs of joyful delight in you as our Father to match your songs of uncontainable enjoyment over us as your children. We pray this for your glory and our good, in Jesus' name, Amen!

The Essential of Faith

Faith is central to the Christian life. Here is a taste of what I mean:

Hebrews 11:6, "Without faith it is impossible to please God, for whoever would draw near to God must believe that he exists and that he rewards those who seek him."

Ephesians 2:8, "For by grace you have been saved through faith and this is not your own doing; it is the gift of God."

Proverbs 3:5-6 says, "Trust in the Lord with all your heart and lean not on your own understanding. In all your ways acknowledge him and he will make straight your paths."

John 3:16, "For God so loved the world that he gave his only Son that whoever believes in him would not perish but would have eternal life."

Obviously this is just a taste of all that God says about Faith. However we do see from these passages that Faith is a non-negotiable for both knowing God personally and living for him faithfully.

Faith, just like prayer, is rooted in the character and promises of God. God's promises are his gifts to us. It's as if the DNA of every promise of God shouts, "Trust Me, I am Faithful and True."

Isaiah 41:10 gives us a glimpse of this:

"Fear not, for I am with you;
be not dismayed, for I am your God;
I will strengthen you, I will help you, I will uphold you with my righteous right hand."

In Romans 15:13 the apostle Paul offers a prayer rooted in faith that I think would be advantageous for all of us to embrace. It goes like this:

"May the God of hope fill you with all joy and peace in **believing**, so that by the power of the Holy Spirit you may abound in Hope."

Our God is the "God of Hope", and he is on a mission to fill us with all joy and peace as we believe his promises. He does all this so that we would ultimately "Abound in Hope by the power of the Holy Spirit."

God wants his people from every generation to be joyful, peaceful and hopeful through faith in him.

A Prayer for Faith

Father, thank you that you are our God of hope! That you are faithful and true in all that you say and do. Cause us to be filled with all joy and peace, as we believe your promises. Cause us by the power of your Holy

Spirit to be people of abounding hope. In your mercy help us to trust and treasure you in all of life. We pray this in Jesus' name, Amen.

The Essential of Purity

Jesus said, "Blessed are the pure in heart for they shall see God." As you pray for your grandchildren, you must aim your prayers at their hearts, because you want them to see God.

You can pray aiming at their hearts in at least two ways: For their *positional purity* before God and for their *practical purity* in becoming like Jesus in this life.

In the Gospel, God takes what is not pure, holy or righteous, i.e. you and me, and makes us perfectly pure through faith in Jesus and his sacrifice on the cross. He longs to do the same for each of your grandchildren.

2 Corinthians 5:21 says it this way: "God made him [Jesus] who had no sin to be sin for us, so that in him we might become the righteousness of God." (NIV)

That's the Gospel! The Great Exchange! Our sin for Christ's righteousness. This is what I mean by positional purity before God.

So, what about our *practical purity*? *Practical purity* is the fight of faith. It is the fight to believe the promises of God over the promises of sin and Satan. Every day you need to remember that our enemy seeks only to steal, kill and destroy our lives and the lives of every young person through the promises of sin and its fleeting pleasures.

With that in mind, I want to highlight three passages to encourage us in our prayers for *practical purity*:

1. Psalm 119:9 "How can a young man (or woman) keep their way pure? By guarding it according to your word." The Word of God is absolutely vital for daily *practical purity*.

2. Proverbs 4:23 "Watch over your heart with all diligence for from it flow the springs of life." Protecting the heart must be a primary concern in daily *practical purity*.
3. 1 John 1:9 "If we confess our sins, he is faithful and just to forgive us our sins and cleanse us from all unrighteousness." *Practical purity* requires regular ongoing personal confession.

As you pray for your grandchildren and each emerging generation, it is essential that we seek God's favor to cause their wisdom, love, faith, and purity to flourish.

A Prayer for Purity

Father, thank you for Jesus! Thank you that he makes us perfectly pure in your sight. Thank you for your Word and its power to guard and guide us in living faithfully for you. Awaken our hearts to your greatness and help us to be relentless in watching over our hearts. In your mercy help us to be people who confess our sins quickly, knowing that you are faithful and just to forgive us and cleanse us from all unrighteousness. We pray this for your glory and our good, in Jesus' name, Amen.

The PR Pair: Speech and Conduct

I love watching the award-winning specials produced by National Geographic. The clarity of nature that they are able to capture is stunning. I am specifically reminded of a photograph of an iceberg in Pleneau Bay off Pleneau Island, which is close to the Antarctic Circle. The photograph was a split shot view capturing a unique image of the iceberg both above and below the waterline. It brought the phrase "tip of the iceberg" to life. Scientists state that because of the density of ice, only ten percent of an iceberg is visible above water, while the bulk of its substance sits below the surface. When you think about it, we are actually a lot like icebergs. People around us get to see about ten percent of who we really are through our speech and conduct—yet there is so much more to us that is "under the waterline". Keep this in mind as you pray, connect and care for your grandchildren.

We were created by God to magnify his greatness by our lips and by our lives.

Let's take a look at both Speech and Conduct individually to finish out our overview of the 7 Essentials.

The Essential of Speech

Words are powerful. Words are literally what God used to create the universe. God cares about the words we use and he wants us to care as much as he does.

In Matthew 12, Jesus gives us a glimpse into why God cares so much about our speech. He says: "For out of the abundance of the heart the mouth speaks." Both the things we say out loud and the things we say in our minds that no one actually hears shine a spotlight on the condition of our hearts.

God cares about our speech because he cares about our hearts. But that's not all, Jesus also says: "I tell you, on the day of judgement people will give account for every careless word they speak, for by your words you will be justified, and by your words you will be condemned."

Those are stunning words from the lips of Jesus declaring that our words really do matter. Our speech actually has eternal implications, not just for ourselves but for those around us as well. Of course the Bible has a lot to say about the power of speech.

Here is a sampling from the book of Proverbs.
- "A gentle answer turns away wrath" 15:1a
- "Rash words are like sword thrusts" 12:18a
- "The tongue of the wise brings healing" 12:18b
- "The mouth of the righteous is a fountain of life" 10:11a
- "Whoever guards his mouth preserves his life" 13:3a

Our words really do matter. As you think about the needs of your grandchildren, some of the greatest words you could ever speak are the words you speak to God on their behalf: your prayers.

May God use your prayers to be a fountain of life for each of your grandchildren and every young person in your lives.

A Prayer for Speech

Father, thank you that you are the creator of language. That your words brought the universe and all it contains into existence. We pray that you would speak into our lives and transform our hearts, causing our speech to bring blessing, healing and life wherever we go. May the words of our mouths and the meditations of our hearts be acceptable in your sight. We pray this for your glory and our good. In Jesus' name, Amen.

The Essential of Conduct

Our conduct is our behavior. It is how we live our lives before God and everyone else. However, it is also an indicator of what is actually happening inside each of us. It's a reflection of our hearts, both the good and the bad.

As you pray for your grandchildren through the lens of conduct, you are praying for all that God is doing deep inside their hearts to be made visible in their conduct. This is why we spend so much time praying for and pursuing the **favor** of God concerning

wisdom, love, faith and **purity**. It is because we know that what is on the inside of each of us eventually comes out in the way we live, in our conduct.

So, the implication is this, if the qualities of **wisdom, love, faith** and **purity** are weak and small in your grandchildren then their conduct will tend to be unwise, unloving, fearful and impure. When this happens it is ultimately a loss for everyone involved.

But here is the good news: You, just like your grandchildren, are not on your own in this journey. Here are three passages to encourage us:

- Philippians 1:6 says, "He who began a good work in you will bring it to completion". God is at work in your grandchildren and he uses your prayers to accomplish his purposes.
- Ephesians 2:10 says it this way , "We are his workmanship, created in Christ for good works which God prepared beforehand that we should walk in them."
- Micah 6:8 echoes Ephesians 2:10 when it says, "He has told you , O man, what is good and what does the Lord require of you but to do justice, and to love kindness, and to walk humbly with your God."

When all is said and done, you want your grandchildren to live lives that are in tune with the purposes of God. You want them to be filled with the Spirit and for their lives to bear the fruit of the Spirit. May God use your prayers to help them blaze a trail for his glory and the good of others with their conduct. May all of our lives leave this kind of legacy.

A Prayer for Conduct

Father, thank you that we are your workmanship, that we are your masterpieces in the making. Help us to walk humbly with you as we seek to do justice and love kindness in this world. Cause us to be relentless in pursuing your Favor to grow deep in Wisdom, Love, Faith and Purity so that our Speech and Conduct would encourage others and exalt you. We pray this for your glory and our good, in Jesus' name, Amen.

The See•Savor•Share Discipleship Process

Life with God is an abundant adventure. It's how he designed it. John 10:10 says, "I came that you might have life and have it abundantly." As you launch into this prayer guide, I want to introduce you to a simple process that can infuse a new freshness into your relationship with God. It's not a panacea or cure all for the difficult days of our lives, but it can definitely strengthen your relationship with God to sustain you in the hard times. I call it the See, Savor, Share discipleship process. The See, Savor, Share discipleship process is the third component that makes this prayer guide unique. Over the last several decades See, Savor, Share has become the rhythm of my life with God, and I would like to encourage you to embrace it as your own as well. At this point it might be helpful to give a little background concerning the value and necessity of See, Savor, Share.

I have been a follower of Christ since 1978, but in March of 1995 the trajectory of my spiritual growth was forever altered. It was then that my wife began having severe, non-stop, relentless migraine-like headaches. Over the next twenty-five-plus years, with three major surgeries and fifty-plus doctors from all across the country in our rearview mirror, her chronic pain has expanded to include intense muscle and bone pain that has caused countless tear-filled nights. For 12 of those years she was mostly bedridden with diminishing thinking abilities and short term memory loss. It was as if she had the symptoms of Alzheimer's even though she didn't have that dreaded disease. Those 12 years are what my family refers to as the "Dark Ages". Those dozen years were crucial years that encompassed my twin daughters' middle school, high school and college years.

It was in this extended season of suffering that I had to learn to walk with God in a new way. The truth is that anyone can live for God on vacation when the wind is at his or her back and all is well. As you can imagine this has not been a vacation. I was constantly being called on as a husband, father and non-profit ministry leader to be more than I had capacity to fulfill. I needed God differently and more desperately than I ever had before.

It was in this setting that the See, Savor, Share discipleship process was born. The See, Savor, Share discipleship process became, and still is, my spiritual survival process. Here is how it works. It is both simple and radical at the same time. It is simple because it is centered on seeing God and his greatness in scripture, life and creation, savoring the greatness of God you have seen for all it is worth and sharing it with others along the way. See, Savor, Share is radical because every moment that is focused on seeing, savoring and sharing the greatness of God is transformational. Over the next few pages I will introduce you to the process, but do not be deceived by its simplicity. Use it to let God saturate you with himself.

Thankfully, you do not have to experience twenty-five plus years of suffering to enjoy the benefits of the See, Savor, Share process. You can begin seeing, savoring, and sharing the greatness of God that is all around you today. See, Savor, Share is the intentional process of looking for God in all of life. It is a thrilling way to walk with

God and fuel a lavish love for him and others, regardless of your circumstances. It is God's desire for us to see his goodness, kindness, mercy, faithfulness, and love in all of life's situations. As he gives us a vision of his greatness in our lives, we must savor it for all it is worth with thanksgiving, praise, and adoration. It is out of the overflow of our savoring that we share freely with others daily. This process can send new life deep into your soul, just as taking in oxygen brings life to the body. See, Savor, Share can become the rhythm of your life with God.

SEE — THE GREATNESS OF GOD — SAVOR — SHARE

At the very core of See, Savor, Share are three powerful truths:
1. Everything God does is great, so everything we see about who God is, what he is doing, or has done should be savored and shared.
2. We can see the greatness of God in Scripture, our daily lives, and in all of creation.
3. The Bible is the only reliable source for understanding what is true about God and what he is doing in our lives and the world around us.

Seeing

Seeing the greatness of God is the first step. The greatness of his character and works can be seen all around us. It is God's desire that we see all of the various aspects of his greatness. He wants our hearts and minds to be captured by the magnificence of his holiness, justice, righteousness, power, wisdom, goodness, patience, kindness, faithfulness, gentleness, and love. His wonders are endless! If our relationship with God ever grows stale, it is not because he is not grand enough to capture the expanse of our hearts; it is because we are blind to the fullness of his beauty. Just as blind Bartimaeus diligently pursued Jesus to give him sight (Mark 10:46-52), so must we be intentional in asking God to give us spiritual sight to see his greatness all around us. Here are some things to remember about seeing God's greatness:

- We can see his greatness in Scripture, life, and creation.
- We can see, hear, and understand what he empowers us to, so one of our constant prayers must be for God to give us eyes to see, ears to hear, and hearts to understand his will and working in this world.

Savoring

Savoring the greatness of God that we see in Scripture, life, and creation is the next step of See, Savor, Share. Savoring is the heart's response to what we are seeing of God. Savoring is essential to our growth with God because it is about enjoying and delighting in God and his greatness. Savoring moves us away from simply having intellectual knowledge of God; it moves us closer to personally knowing him and what he cares about. It moves us closer because sustained savoring expands our heart's capacity to love God. Here are some things to remember about savoring God's greatness:

- Savoring is essential because we pursue what we love with purpose and intensity.

- Savoring takes time. We have to slow down and ponder what we have seen.
- Giving thanks, delighting, and treasuring are key aspects of savoring.
- Begin savoring by recalling times or places in your life where you have seen God's presence, protection, or provision.

Sharing

Sharing about God is the natural overflow of seeing and savoring his greatness. Sharing actually plays two primary roles for us in our growth with God. First, it completes the enjoyment of what we have seen and savored. When we see something incredible, we immediately begin looking for someone to share it with. Sharing is the culminating point in enjoying the greatness of God we have seen. Second, sharing helps us see what has a hold on our hearts. We naturally talk about what we love and enjoy. See, Savor, Share is designed to help us deepen our love and enjoyment in God by seeing, savoring, and ultimately sharing his greatness with others. Here are a few things to remember about sharing God's greatness:

- Pay attention to what you talk about most. This can give you some insight into what holds the most space in your heart. The goal in this process is that you would begin to see and savor the greatness of God in your life, and sharing would naturally become the next step.
- To begin sharing, engage others about where they have seen God at work in their lives. Most people will have a time or place where they would say God has worked in their life.
- Be prepared to share stories about how you've seen God's greatness in your life. Sharing deepens your relationship

with God in Christ. Philemon 6 says, "I pray that the sharing of your faith may become effective for the full knowledge of every good thing that is in us for the sake of Christ." This is a great encouragement and promise! This means every time we ask someone to share how God has worked in their lives, we are providing a means of establishing them in their faith. So don't hesitate to share, and don't hesitate to ask others to share!

See, Savor, Share is included in this prayer guide to bring the abstract truth about God into the present reality of your life. When you pray for your grandchildren, you must remember to pray with a vision of their being captured by the greatness of God. Each day you will pray one of The 7 Essentials using the See, Savor, Share process as your lens to help provide focus and clarity for these prayers. May God grant us favor to see and savor his greatness in Scripture, life, and creation, so we will be ready to share it to each emerging generation.

Make the Prayers Your Own!

As you begin your journey through the prayers in this guide, remember to make them your own! Each prayer is written in plural form to allow you ease in praying for several or all of your grandchildren at once. I realize that you may only have one grandchild. Don't let the plural language throw you off. Here are two options: 1) Feel free to add other young people you care about from your church or neighborhood into your prayers to make them plural. Or, 2) you can just make the adjustment to the singular in your mind as you pray. Also, there may be a tendency to read through the prayers in a rote manner; resist this tendency. Take time to hover over the words and phrases and let their meaning soak into your soul.

Finally, find freedom in expanding and enhancing the prayers as you offer them to God. Enjoy the adventure of interceding for your grands. The world will be different because of your prayers.

PRAY for ME CAMPAIGN SPOTLIGHT

Susan's Kids

This church like many was siloed off by generation.

Its members exposed this division by casually referring to their students as "Susan's kids". They assumed this one youth leader Susan was responsible for the spiritual development of all of their students.

However, when Susan launched the Pray for Me Campaign, it naturally created relationships across generational lines when students each invited three adults from different generations to be their prayer champions.

One year later, many other adults alongside Susan were invested in their youth as their prayer champions, no longer calling them "Susan's kids" but "our kids".

Through the Pray for Me Campaign, this church took ownership of their youth because they now knew them personally and desired to make a difference in their lives.

PART TWO

The 7 Essentials in 7 Days

Every day is designed to provide you with a clear and fresh opportunity for engaging God in Scripture through prayer for your grandchildren. It is my hope that you will pray for your grandchildren as well as anyone God may put on your heart.

The See, Savor, Share discipleship process guides you through each day, prompting you with ways to see, savor, and share the fullness of God. The *see* portion is a passage of Scripture where you can circle or underline words and phrases that stand out to you. Next, you will *savor* those truths in prayer for your grandchildren. Finally, you will have the opportunity to record any thoughts or ideas that were pressed into your heart during the see and savor portions. It is my hope and expectation that you will *share* them with your grandchildren in a winsome and natural way!

Day One: Favor

Father, open my eyes so that I might *see* you more clearly, *savor* you more fully, and *share* you more freely.

Circle or underline any key words or phrases you **See**:

Yours, O LORD, is the greatness and the power and the glory and the victory and the majesty, for all that is in the heavens and in the earth is yours. Yours is the kingdom, O LORD, and you are exalted as head above all. Both riches and honor come from you, and you rule over all. In your hand are power and might, and in your hand it is to make great and to give strength to all. And now we thank you, our God, and praise your glorious name. (1 Chronicles 29:11-13)

Savor these truths in prayer:

Father, you are great and worthy to be praised. I pray that _____ would know and embrace your favor and never stop growing in wonder and amazement of your greatness. Awaken their hearts and minds to comprehend that all goodness flows from your hand. When they look at the heavens, cause them to know the heavens are yours! When they look in the mirror, cause them to know that they are yours. Create in them a relentless reliance on you and your provisions of favor in all of life. Enable them to be enthralled by you as the giver of all things. Give them deep enjoyment and thankfulness at the thought of your glorious name. For your glory and their good, in the sovereign name of Jesus, amen.

Write down any thoughts or ideas you may want to **Share**:

Day Two: Wisdom

Father, open my eyes so that I might *see* you more clearly, *savor* you more fully, and *share* you more freely.

Circle or underline any key words or phrases you **See**:

So teach us to number our days that we may get a heart of wisdom. (Psalm 90:12)

O Lord, make me know my end and what is the measure of my days; let me know how fleeting I am! (Psalm 39:4)

Savor these truths in prayer:

> Father, it is so easy for days and years to pass by before we realize they are gone. I pray for _____, that you would help them realize how precious each moment is. Teach them to savor every day as a gift from you and help them to live each day with purposeful intentionality. Cause them to understand that their lives are sustained by you. Help them to realize this life is also fleeting, so they should always seek to follow you faithfully. Give them a long-term view of life so they can make wise short-term decisions. Remind them that it is in living for you that their lives become the most fulfilling. For your glory and their good, in Jesus' name, amen.

Write down any thoughts or ideas you may want to **Share**:

Day Three: Love

Father, open my eyes so that I might *see* you more clearly, *savor* you more fully, and *share* you more freely.

Circle or underline any key words or phrases you **See**:

For God so loved the world, that he gave his only Son, that whoever believes in him should not perish but have eternal life. (John 3:16)

For while we were still weak, at the right time Christ died for the ungodly. For one will scarcely die for a righteous person—though perhaps for a good person one would dare even to die—but God shows his love for us in that while we were still sinners, Christ died for us. (Romans 5:6-8)

Savor these truths in prayer:

> Father, thank you for showing us what perfect love looks like in Jesus. I pray that in your grace and mercy you would grant _____ eyes to see the scope and uniqueness of your love. It is not earned, but received by faith. Cause their hearts and minds to be captured by your relentless, sacrificial and personal love for them in Jesus. Create in each of them a tenacious trust and treasuring of Jesus alone for their salvation. Give them an unshakable confidence that eternal life is found in Jesus alone, through faith alone. By your grace, empower them to live sacrificial loving lives. For your glory and their good, in Jesus' name, amen.

Write down any thoughts or ideas you may want to **Share**:

Day Four: Faith

Father, open my eyes so that I might *see* you more clearly, *savor* you more fully, and *share* you more freely.

Circle or underline any key words or phrases you **See**:

Trust in the LORD with all your heart, and do not lean on your own understanding. In all your ways acknowledge him, and he will make straight your paths. (Proverbs 3:5-6)

Savor these truths in prayer:

> Father, life is so often complex and confusing. I thank you for your promises that provide hope and clarity in the midst of life's complexity. Today I pray that _____ would place their trust in you, surrendering every aspect of their lives to you, believing that you love them. Empower them to fight the urge to trust in their own understanding more than they rely on you and your guidance. Cause them to look to you in all their ways, acknowledging their need for, dependence on, and hope in you. Help them to acknowledge all of your provisions as they see you make their paths straight. Give them eyes to see the wonders you perform as they surrender and yield to your purposes. You are their God! Help them treasure you today with every breath, and cause them to call others to treasure you with all of their hearts as well. For your glory and their good, in Jesus' name, amen!

Write down any thoughts or ideas you may want to **Share**:

Day Five: Purity

Father, open my eyes so that I might *see* you more clearly, *savor* you more fully, and *share* you more freely.

Circle or underline any key words or phrases you **See**:

How can a young man keep his way pure? By guarding it according to your word. With my whole heart I seek you; let me not wander from your commandments! I have stored up your word in my heart, that I might not sin against you. (Psalm 119:9-11)

Savor these truths in prayer:

> Father, in a world that disregards purity, the question of the psalmist is vital: "How can a young man [or woman] keep their way pure?" By listening, loving and living according to what you say is the answer. I pray that _____ would taste the sweetness of Scripture and that their hearts would overflow with enjoyment. Help them to feast on the wonders of your word daily like they feed on food. Use the power of your Word, the Sword of the Spirit, to lead, guide, and empower them to pursue purity and holiness in every decision. Give them a steadfast desire and will to treasure your Word in their hearts so that their lives bring you honor and glory. Holy, holy, holy is the Lord God Almighty. In Jesus' name, amen.

Write down any thoughts or ideas you may want to **Share**:

Day Six: Speech

Father, open my eyes so that I might *see* you more clearly, *savor* you more fully, and *share* you more freely.

Circle or underline any key words or phrases you **See**:

It is good to give thanks to the LORD, to sing praises to your name, O Most High; to declare your steadfast love in the morning, and your faithfulness by night... (Psalm 92:1-2)

Savor these truths in prayer:

Father, I praise you today. You are great and glorious. Help _____ to use their words to give you thanks and praise for all you are and all you do. Let their hearts overflow with songs of praise to your name. Give them understanding of your great love for them each morning and let their words declare your steadfast love. Help them to see and savor the truth that every day they are walking into the care and love of their heavenly Father. Grant them the ability to recognize your faithfulness throughout each day, using their speech to tell the world about your greatness. For your glory and their good, in Jesus' name, amen.

Write down any thoughts or ideas you may want to **Share**:

Day Seven: Conduct

Father, open my eyes so that I might *see* you more clearly, *savor* you more fully, and *share* you more freely.

Circle or underline any key words or phrases you **See**:

He has told you, O man, what is good; and what does the LORD require of you but to do justice, and to love kindness, and to walk humbly with your God? (Micah 6:8)

Savor these truths in prayer:

> Father, thank you for telling us what is good in this life along with the things you require of us to honor your name. I pray that _____ would learn to love what you require of them. Make their hearts tender and responsive to all of your commands to do justice, love kindness, and walk humbly with you all of their days. Awaken their hearts and minds to the needs for love and mercy all around them. Give them the wisdom, abilities, and tenacious desire required to meet those needs. Give them eyes to see the world the way you see it and grant them the courage to stand against injustice for your glory and the good of those being mistreated. As they seek to promote justice and to love kindness in this world, empower them to do it with humility before you and man. For your glory and their good, in Jesus' name, amen.

Write down any thoughts or ideas you may want to **Share**:

Notes

WEEK TWO

The 7 Essentials in 7 Days

By now you are getting into the rhythm of praying for your grandchildren. You have just prayed a week of the 7 Essentials over them. Only God knows the extent of goodness he is bringing their way because of your prayers. As you begin praying a second week for your grandchildren, remember to pay attention to what God brings to the forefront of your mind. I tend to see these prayers as "spark" prayers. God can use these prayers as a spark of his goodness to ignite a blaze of ongoing prayer for your grandchildren and others throughout the day. Let any thoughts or ideas you may have prompt you to drill down deeper in prayer. It could be that at the end of each prayer you ask yourself:

What one thing would I add to this prayer for my grandchildren?
Or:
What is today's takeaway thought for ongoing prayer?

Day One: Favor

Father, open my eyes so that I might *see* you more clearly, *savor* you more fully, and *share* you more freely.

Circle or underline any key words or phrases you **See**:

For by grace you have been saved through faith. And this is not your own doing; it is the gift of God, not a result of works, so that no one may boast. For we are his workmanship, created in Christ Jesus for good works, which God prepared beforehand, that we should walk in them. (Ephesians 2:8-10)

Savor these truths in prayer:

> Father, thank you that salvation is a gift. Thank you that it is not based on our good works, but on Jesus' perfect work on the cross. I pray that you would give _____ faith to trust you alone for their salvation. Give them your abiding peace that comes from knowing your perfect love, which you displayed in Jesus' death, burial, and resurrection. Cause them to know how amazingly special they are as your workmanship, created in Jesus Christ to do good works as a result of their salvation, not in order to gain it. Empower them to relentlessly pursue the good works you have prepared for them to accomplish. For your glory and their good, in the precious name of Christ, amen.

Write down any thoughts or ideas you may want to ***Share***:

Day Two: Wisdom

Father, open my eyes so that I might *see* you more clearly, *savor* you more fully, and *share* you more freely.

Circle or underline any key words or phrases you **See**:

And he said to man, "Behold, the fear of the Lord, that is wisdom, and to turn away from evil is understanding." (Job 28:28)

The fear of the Lord is the beginning of wisdom; all those who practice it have a good understanding. His praise endures forever! (Psalm 111:10)

Savor these truths in prayer:

> Father, you are wise and wonderful in all you are and do. I pray today that _____ would fear you in a way that matches your worth. Cause them to see you and themselves accurately, which produces in them a fear of you that is full of deep respect, honor, and adoration. Create in them a humble dependence on you for all things. Give them deep satisfaction and joy in turning away from evil in both small and big things. Cause their minds to be filled with insight and understanding concerning the pursuit of the paths of righteousness. Remove the obstacles that blind and deceive them from recognizing your perfect and sovereign work in this world. Make their hearts overflow with praise and thankfulness for all your goodness in their lives. Strengthen them in their ability to help others see your greatness. For your glory and their good, in Jesus' all-wise and wonderful name, amen.

Write down any thoughts or ideas you may want to **Share**:

Day Three: Love

Father, open my eyes so that I might *see* you more clearly, *savor* you more fully, and *share* you more freely.

Circle or underline any key words or phrases you **See**:

And he said to him, "You shall love the Lord your God with all your heart and with all your soul and with all your mind. This is the great and first commandment. And a second is like it: You shall love your neighbor as yourself. On these two commandments depend all the Law and the Prophets." (Matthew 22:37-40)

Savor these truths in prayer:

> Father, thank you that your greatest command is for our greatest good. I pray that _____ would seek to love you with all of their heart, soul, and mind. Cause them to find their greatest delight in you. Give them understanding that their deepest desires can only be satisfied by loving you in all they say, think, and do. Do not let them grow weary in their pursuit to love you supremely. Protect them from the temptation to settle for lesser loves. Capture them with the magnificence of your love for them and cause them to be tenacious in loving others as themselves. Let their lives be a constant demonstration of your love to the world. For your glory and their good, in the wonderful name of Jesus, amen.

Write down any thoughts or ideas you may want to **Share**:

Day Four: Faith

Father, open my eyes so that I might *see* you more clearly, *savor* you more fully, and *share* you more freely.

Circle or underline any key words or phrases you **See**:

I know that you can do all things, and that no purpose of yours can be thwarted. (Job 42:2)

Ah, Lord GOD! It is you who have made the heavens and the earth by your great power and by your outstretched arm! Nothing is too hard for you..."Behold, I am the LORD, the God of all flesh. Is anything too hard for me?" (Jeremiah 32:17, 27)

Savor these truths in prayer:

> Father, life is filled with challenges and limitations that whisper and sometimes even shout at us saying we are not enough, and yet we rest in knowing that you are more than enough for everything we face in this life. I pray for _____ today, that you would give them faith in your ability to do all things. Help them to believe that there is no purpose of yours that can be thwarted. Help them learn the great stories in your Word that show your faithfulness in difficult times. When they are faced with impossible challenges, remind them that nothing is too hard for you. Assure them that you work everything for the good of those who love you, so that they might be conformed into the image of your Son. May you be praised forever! In Jesus' name, amen.

Write down any thoughts or ideas you may want to **Share**:

Day Five: Purity

Father, open my eyes so that I might *see* you more clearly, *savor* you more fully, and *share* you more freely.

Circle or underline any key words or phrases you **See**:

I have made a covenant with my eyes; how then could I gaze at a virgin? (Job 31:1)

Sheol and Abaddon are never satisfied, and never satisfied are the eyes of man. (Proverbs 27:20)

Savor these truths in prayer:

> Father, as I pray for _____ and their purity today, I ask that you would make them alert to the people, places, and things that they look upon. Help them to be like Job and make a covenant with their eyes, guarding their gaze and not looking at others inappropriately. Help them to diligently seek purity. Help them to understand that their purity can be fueled or foiled by the direction of their gaze. Protect them from the futility of trying to be satisfied by what they see. The eyes of man cannot be satisfied apart from you. You alone can create in them a satisfaction that supersedes all lures or lusts that come before their eyes. For your glory and their good, in Jesus' name, amen.

Write down any thoughts or ideas you may want to ***Share***:

Day Six: Speech

Father, open my eyes so that I might *see* you more clearly, *savor* you more fully, and *share* you more freely.

Circle or underline any key words or phrases you **See**:

One generation shall commend your works to another, and shall declare your mighty acts. On the glorious splendor of your majesty, and on your wondrous works, I will meditate. They shall speak of the might of your awesome deeds, and I will declare your greatness. (Psalm 145:4-6)

Savor these truths in prayer:

> Father, help _____ to know that the deepest and most profound longing of their hearts is to know and love you. To taste and see your greatness daily in their lives. Today I pray for myself and a whole host of other adults who have seen and savored your greatness. Bring these adults into my grandchildren's lives. Give them courage to take the initiative to care and share the greatness that you have displayed in their lives. Give my grandchildren ears to hear and hearts to understand and delight in all that you have done. Grant that these stories of your greatness will fill them with relentless hope. In your mercy, cause them to begin seeing, savoring, and sharing their own stories of your greatness with others. For your glory and their good, in Jesus' name, amen.

Write down any thoughts or ideas you may want to **Share**:

Day Seven: Conduct

Father, open my eyes so that I might *see* you more clearly, *savor* you more fully, and *share* you more freely.

Circle or underline any key words or phrases you **See**:

"This Book of the Law shall not depart from your mouth, but you shall meditate on it day and night, so that you may be careful to do according to all that is written in it. For then you will make your way prosperous, and then you will have good success. Have I not commanded you? Be strong and courageous. Do not be frightened, and do not be dismayed, for the LORD your God is with you wherever you go." (Joshua 1:8-9)

Savor these truths in prayer:

> Father, I praise you and thank you for the promises in your Word. I pray that _____ would take hold of your Word with all their hearts and minds. Give them a craving for your Word that causes them to read, memorize, and meditate on it day and night. Cause them to care about all that you command and be quick to obey you out of a heart of love, knowing your promises of goodness will follow. Create in them a courageous and strong resolve to pursue all that you desire for them. Don't let fear cause them to falter. Fill them with faith to believe they can go anywhere you command. Give them a sense of your powerful presence to strengthen them to pursue your purposes with courage. For your glory and their good, in Jesus' name, amen.

Write down any thoughts or ideas you may want to **Share**:

Notes

WEEK THREE

The 7 Essentials in 7 Days

Grant me, O Lord my God, a mind to know you, a heart to seek you, wisdom to find you, conduct pleasing to you, faithful perseverance in waiting for you, and a hope of finally embracing you. Amen. — ST. THOMAS AQUINAS

...a spiritual life without prayer is like the gospel without Christ.
— HENRI J.M. NOUWEN

Prayer is an act of brave trust in God. — RHONDA SOUDER

Day One: Favor

Father, open my eyes so that I might *see* you more clearly, *savor* you more fully, and *share* you more freely.

Circle or underline any key words or phrases you **See**:

Let not steadfast love and faithfulness forsake you; bind them around your neck; write them on the tablet of your heart. So you will find favor and good success in the sight of God and man. (Proverbs 3:3-4)

Savor these truths in prayer:

> Father, I pray for _____, that you would lavish them with your favor today. Help them to sense your steadfast love and faithfulness as they go about their day. Cause them to see your goodness and how you have loved and cared for them. Give them opportunities so they can help others know and experience your love and faithfulness today. May their lives be so clearly marked by your love and faithfulness that favor and success would be their constant companions. Cause them to feel your hand of favor on their lives and remind them that where they go the favor of God goes. For your glory and their good, in Jesus' name, amen.

Write down any thoughts or ideas you may want to **Share**:

Day Two: Wisdom

Father, open my eyes so that I might *see* you more clearly, *savor* you more fully, and *share* you more freely.

Circle or underline any key words or phrases you **See**:

Be not wise in your own eyes: fear the LORD, and turn away from evil. (Proverbs 3:7)

Do you see a man who is wise in his own eyes? There is more hope for a fool than for him. (Proverbs 26:12)

Savor these truths in prayer:

> Father, your word is a well of wisdom for all who are teachable. It gives life, hope and direction for all who humble themselves to satisfy themselves in you. I pray today that _____ would walk in humility and look to you for wisdom, truth and hope. Help them fight the temptation to be wise in their own eyes. Grant them grace to appropriately fear and exalt you in their lives. Protect them from the self-exaltation that puts them at the center of life rather than you and the good of others. Cause them to have a profound sense of your greatness, knowing they are accountable to you in all they do, say and think. Fill them with a conviction of right and wrong that leads to a relentless desire to turn from evil quickly and consistently. For your glory and their good, I pray in Jesus' name, amen.

Write down any thoughts or ideas you may want to **Share**:

Day Three: Love

Father, open my eyes so that I might *see* you more clearly, *savor* you more fully, and *share* you more freely.

Circle or underline any key words or phrases you **See**:

For as high as the heavens are above the earth, so great is his steadfast love toward those who fear him; as far as the east is from the west, so far does he remove our transgressions from us. (Psalm 103:11-12)

Savor these truths in prayer:

> Father, I pray that _____ would gain an ever-growing understanding that your love is great toward those who fear you. Stir up within them a sense of awe and respect for you that is unquenchable. As they look at the daytime sky and the night's starry host, cause them to feel the vastness of your love for them that stretches to the highest heavens. Thank you that your love and forgiveness is perfect and complete. Let them feel the freedom of your complete and unending forgiveness through Jesus and his sacrifice every single day. Help them to be open, available and eager to show your love and forgiveness to others every day. For your glory and their good, in Jesus' name, amen.

Write down any thoughts or ideas you may want to **Share**:

Day Four: Faith

Father, open my eyes so that I might *see* you more clearly, *savor* you more fully, and *share* you more freely.

Circle or underline any key words or phrases you **See**:

And those who know your name put their trust in you, for you, O LORD, have not forsaken those who seek you. (Psalm 9:10)

Some trust in chariots and some in horses, but we trust in the name of the LORD our God. (Psalm 20:7)

Savor these truths in prayer:

> Father, your promises are true. You are faithful to those who put their trust in you! I pray for _____, that they would know your character, causing their hearts to grow large with faith and trust in you. Create in them confidence that your name represents all of your authority, power, and greatness. Help them to savor you as their Creator, Sustainer, Provider, Healer, and Redeemer. Take hold of them in such a way that they will passionately seek you, knowing that you will never forsake them. You are the Prince of Peace, so anoint them with your perfect peace. You are the King of Kings, so reign over them in all of your goodness. You are the Great I Am, so give them faith to trust you for all they need. For your glory and their good, in Jesus' name, amen.

Write down any thoughts or ideas you may want to **Share**:

Day Five: Purity

Father, open my eyes so that I might *see* you more clearly, *savor* you more fully, and *share* you more freely.

Circle or underline any key words or phrases you **See**:

Blessed are the pure in heart, for they shall see God.
(Matthew 5:8)

Savor these truths in prayer:

> Father, thank you for this day that you have ordained for _____. I pray for their happiness today. Jesus said that blessed are the pure in heart for they shall see God. Give them uncontainable joy in you. Don't let them miss the wonder and joy of seeing you because they settled for some false promise of pleasure elsewhere. Cause them to be enthralled by a clear vision of your greatness so that every other empty promise of happiness apart from you would be powerless in their hearts. It is by your Spirit that they are empowered to walk in purity. Fill them with your Spirit today. Cause the joy from seeing your magnificence to overflow in blessing and purity to those around them. For your glory and their good, in Jesus' name, amen.

Write down any thoughts or ideas you may want to **Share**:

Day Six: Speech

Father, open my eyes so that I might *see* you more clearly, *savor* you more fully, and *share* you more freely.

Circle or underline any key words or phrases you **See**:

When words are many, transgression is not lacking, but whoever restrains his lips is prudent. (Proverbs 10:19)

There is one whose rash words are like sword thrusts, but the tongue of the wise brings healing. Truthful lips endure forever, but a lying tongue is but for a moment. (Proverbs 12:18-19)

Savor these truths in prayer:

> Father, thank you for giving us the gift of language and the ability to express ourselves with words. I pray that you would bless _____ with wisdom and favor so they can learn to use their words well. Give them wisdom on when to speak and when to keep silent. Protect them from being reckless and rash with their speech, using words that damage and destroy. Cause their words to be filled with wisdom from above, bringing healing everywhere they go. Give them a courageous commitment to always speak the truth in love. Remind them that a lying tongue always comes to an undesirable end. Cause them to be known for the kindness and encouragement they bring with their words. For your glory and their good. In Jesus' name, amen.

Write down any thoughts or ideas you may want to **Share**:

Day Seven: Conduct

Father, open my eyes so that I might *see* you more clearly, *savor* you more fully, and *share* you more freely.

Circle or underline any key words or phrases you **See**:

Good and upright is the LORD; therefore he instructs sinners in the way. He leads the humble in what is right, and teaches the humble his way. All the paths of the LORD are steadfast love and faithfulness, for those who keep his covenant and his testimonies. (Psalm 25:8-10)

Savor these truths in prayer:

Father, thank you that you are good and upright in all you do. Thank you for correcting us when we stray from your truth and instructing us in the way we should go. I pray that you would create in _____ humble hearts that are teachable and responsive to all of your instruction and purposes. Help them to understand that you lead the humble in all that is right and that you teach them to live in your ways. Give them joy in obeying your Word as well as a strong conviction that all of your paths are marked by steadfast love and faithfulness. Cause them to resist living out of pride, knowing that you give grace to the humble. Make your truth their treasure. For your glory and their good, in Jesus' name, amen.

Write down any thoughts or ideas you may want to **Share**:

Notes

WEEK FOUR

The 7 Essentials in 7 Days

My daughter jokes about how she loves to run short distances at a long distance pace. I laugh every time she says it because I identify with it so much. I wonder if we could benefit by applying my daughter's running approach to our prayers. Here is what I mean: Even though they are short prayers, it doesn't mean you should speed through them. Pace yourself. You can even think of it as a prayer stroll. As you are praying, find a word, phrase, or sentence and linger over it for a little while. Don't feel the need to rush to the next sentence. Let God help you savor the elements of each passage and prayer long into the day. Enjoy your stroll.

Day One: Favor

Father, open my eyes so that I might *see* you more clearly, *savor* you more fully, and *share* you more freely.

Circle or underline any key words or phrases you **See**:

...since he himself gives to all mankind life and breath and everything..."in him we live and move and have our being." (Acts 17:25, 28)

What do you have that you did not receive? If then you received it, why do you boast as if you did not receive it? (1 Corinthians 4:7)

Savor these truths in prayer:

> Father, every breath is a gift of your grace and favor. It is from your hand that _____ have life and breath and all things today. Grant them delight in your sustaining favor that makes it possible for them to live and move and have their being. Keep them from taking your enduring goodness and favor to them for granted. Give them eyes to see your sustaining favor and create in them genuine joy for every life-giving breath they breathe by your grace. Make their hearts full with thanksgiving for all your gifts of favor. For your glory and their good, in the all-sustaining name of Jesus, amen.

Write down any thoughts or ideas you may want to **Share**:

Day Two: Wisdom

Father, open my eyes so that I might *see* you more clearly, *savor* you more fully, and *share* you more freely.

Circle or underline any key words or phrases you **See**:

The words of the wise are like goads, and like nails firmly fixed are the collected sayings; they are given by one Shepherd. My son, beware of anything beyond these. Of making many books there is no end, and much study is a weariness of the flesh. The end of the matter; all has been heard. Fear God and keep his commandments, for this is the whole duty of man. For God will bring every deed into judgment, with every secret thing, whether good or evil. (Ecclesiastes 12:11-14)

Savor these truths in prayer:

> Father, thank you for reminding us that wisdom comes from you, the Great Shepherd. I pray that _____ would long to know what you think and say in your Word about how they should live. Give them discernment in deciding where and how to pursue wisdom. Help them to let the biblical proverbs and the parables of Jesus soak deeply into their lives. Cause them to become incredibly wise influencers for your purposes in this world. Strengthen them by the power of your Spirit to honor and obey you in all things, knowing that they are ultimately accountable to you. For your glory and their good, in Jesus' name, amen.

Write down any thoughts or ideas you may want to **Share**:

Day Three: Love

Father, open my eyes so that I might *see* you more clearly, *savor* you more fully, and *share* you more freely.

Circle or underline any key words or phrases you **See**:

Who shall separate us from the love of Christ? Shall tribulation, or distress, or persecution, or famine, or nakedness, or danger, or sword? (Romans 8:35)

For I am sure that neither death nor life, nor angels nor rulers, nor things present nor things to come, nor powers, nor height nor depth, nor anything else in all creation, will be able to separate us from the love of God in Christ Jesus our Lord. (Romans 8:38,39)

Savor these truths in prayer:

> Father, your love is one of your superpowers. Thank you for taking hold of your children with your unbreakable love in Christ. I pray that you would take hold of _____ with your love. Cause them to find their greatest security, confidence, hope and rest in your loving and unshakeable grip. Draw each of them to yourself and embrace them with your everlasting love. With all of the challenges and suffering that this fallen world brings upon them, make them resilient and relentless in fixing their eyes on you and your love for them. Create in them an ever-growing confidence that there is nothing that can defeat your love for them. For your glory and their good, I pray in Jesus' name, amen.

Write down any thoughts or ideas you may want to **Share**:

Day Four: Faith

Father, open my eyes so that I might *see* you more clearly, *savor* you more fully, and *share* you more freely.

Circle or underline any key words or phrases you **See**:

Count it all joy, my brothers, when you meet trials of various kinds, for you know that the testing of your faith produces steadfastness. And let steadfastness have its full effect, that you may be perfect and complete, lacking in nothing. (James 1:2-4)

Savor these truths in prayer:

> Father, your ways are perfect and yet they are so contrary to the ways of the world. I pray that _____ would embrace the paradox of counting it all joy when they encounter trials of all shapes and sizes. May their faith in you be resilient, strong, and persevering as they trust your sovereign goodness in trials. Protect them from the pull to give up and flee from the fight of faith. Remind them that they are not alone, that you are there with them in every trial. Fortify their faith in you, knowing that you are conforming them into the image of your Son, Jesus. Help them to believe that becoming more like Jesus is worth every trial. As gold is refined in fire, let their steadfastness and perseverance in trials have its full impact, that they may be perfect and complete, lacking in nothing. For your glory and their good, in Jesus' name, amen.

Write down any thoughts or ideas you may want to **Share**:

Day Five: Purity

Father, open my eyes so that I might *see* you more clearly, *savor* you more fully, and *share* you more freely.

Circle or underline any key words or phrases you **See**:

Keep your heart with all vigilance, for from it flow the springs of life. (Proverbs 4:23)

And he said, "What comes out of a person is what defiles him. For from within, out of the heart of man, come evil thoughts, sexual immorality, theft, murder, adultery, coveting, wickedness, deceit, sensuality, envy, slander, pride, foolishness. All these evil things come from within, and they defile a person." (Mark 7:20-23)

Savor these truths in prayer:

> Father, in our pursuit of following you in faithfulness and becoming like you in holiness, we realize that some actions are more important than others. Guarding our hearts is one of those vital acts. I pray that _____ would exercise vigilance in guarding their heart by the power of your Spirit. Help them to see the places where they need to protect their heart better. Help them to find friends that will strengthen their resolve to guard their hearts. Cause them to see with clarity the disappointing consequences of people who live with unguarded hearts. Fill them with your Spirit so that rivers of living water will flow out of them. For your glory and their good, in Jesus' name, amen.

Write down any thoughts or ideas you may want to **Share**:

Day Six: Speech

Father, open my eyes so that I might *see* you more clearly, *savor* you more fully, and *share* you more freely.

Circle or underline any key words or phrases you **See**:

A soft answer turns away wrath, but a harsh word stirs up anger. The tongue of the wise commends knowledge, but the mouths of fools pour out folly...A gentle tongue is a tree of life, but perverseness in it breaks the spirit. (Proverbs 15:1-2, 4)

Savor these truths in prayer:

> Father, thank you for the power of soft and gentle speech. I pray that you would provide _____ with people who would lavish them with the goodness of soft and gentle speech. In the same way I pray that they would be generous in offering up words that are soft and gentle to others. Cause the fruit of their words to be a tree of life, turning away wrath and anger. Let wisdom flow from their lips, commending knowledge that is life-giving to all who hear. Protect them from giving or receiving harsh words that stir up anger or hate. Give them the ability to graciously change the subject when perverse speech breaks out around them. Do not let evil and harsh words be used to harm them in any way. Help them to embrace your truth so they can overcome any false words directed toward them. For your glory and their good, in Jesus' name, amen.

Write down any thoughts or ideas you may want to **Share**:

Day Seven: Conduct

Father, open my eyes so that I might *see* you more clearly, *savor* you more fully, and *share* you more freely.

Circle or underline any key words or phrases you **See**:

Be appalled, O heavens, at this; be shocked, be utterly desolate, declares the LORD, for my people have committed two evils: they have forsaken me, the fountain of living waters, and hewed out cisterns for themselves, broken cisterns that can hold no water. (Jeremiah 2:12-13)

Savor these truths in prayer:

> Father, thank you that you are the fountain of living waters and the only place we can be perfectly satisfied. I pray that _____ would fully and completely believe that you are enough to satisfy their hearts. Make them alert to the slightest tendencies to turn away from you to find happiness somewhere else. Cause them to see and understand how appalling and shocking it is for your children to reject you to find joy and life somewhere else. Help them to flee the futility of trying to find happiness through their own devices. Forgive them when they think about or pursue you in a casual way. Create in them a craving for you and your ways that surpasses every promise of pleasure in other things. Strengthen them to help those around them to turn away from their futile ways and find fullness of joy in you. For your glory and their good, in Jesus' name, amen.

Write down any thoughts or ideas you may want to **Share**:

Notes

WEEK FIVE

The 7 Essentials in 7 Days

"*My grandmother, Miss Lucy, was the greatest influence in my life during my adolescence.*"
— BARRY ST. CLAIR

"Tell me someone who is a life-giving presence for you." That was the question that Jane Henegar asked her class of high school girls. The answer came quickly for one of the girls as if in her mind she said, "That's easy, it's my GiGi!" Her grandmother immediately came to her mind.

When I hear stories like this, something strange begins to happen to me. My heart begins to pound and my mind begins to race, because I realize that I want to be like GiGi! I want to love others well and breathe life into them. A great starting place for being this kind of person is prayer.

Day One: Favor

Father, open my eyes so that I might *see* you more clearly, *savor* you more fully, and *share* you more freely.

Circle or underline any key words or phrases you **See**:

The LORD is gracious and merciful, slow to anger and abounding in steadfast love. The LORD is good to all, and his mercy is over all that he has made. (Psalm 145:8,9)

Savor these truths in prayer:

> Father, thank you for your all-encompassing favor. Thank you that you are good to all and your mercy is over all that you have made, which includes my grandchildren. I pray today that _____ would sense your goodness and mercy toward them. Help me to remember that every prayer I pray for them is a portion of your goodness and mercy over their lives. Give them eyes to see that the origin of every provision in their lives is the result of you opening your hand to satisfy the desire of every living thing. Cause them to know, enjoy and delight in your goodness and mercy. Make them resilient in trusting and treasuring you in every moment. Fuel their hearts and minds with relentless thankfulness for all of the goodness and mercy that you provide each day. For your glory and their good, in Jesus' name I pray, amen.

Write down any thoughts or ideas you may want to **Share**:

Day Two: Wisdom

Father, open my eyes so that I might *see* you more clearly, *savor* you more fully, and *share* you more freely.

Circle or underline any key words or phrases you **See**:

Do not reprove a scoffer, or he will hate you; reprove a wise man, and he will love you. Give instruction to a wise man, and he will be wiser still; teach a righteous man, and he will increase in learning. (Proverbs 9:8,9)

Savor these truths in prayer:

> Father, you are great and glorious in all that you are and do. Thank you that wisdom and righteousness are some of your greatest gifts to your children. Today I pray that _____ would be wise in all they do. Cause them to be responsive and teachable to correction and instruction. Give them a keen awareness of the state of their hearts before you and others. It is so easy for symptoms of hard-heartedness and stubbornness to seep into our lives. Help them see the symptoms in their lives and in your mercy cause them to confess and forsake every whiff of rebellion that may be hiding in their hearts. Make them the poster children for being teachable when corrected. Stir up within them the desire to be wise and to have wise people in their lives that will help them follow you faithfully for a lifetime. For your glory and their good, in Jesus' name I pray, amen.

Write down any thoughts or ideas you may want to **Share**:

Day Three: Love

Father, open my eyes so that I might *see* you more clearly, *savor* you more fully, and *share* you more freely.

Circle or underline any key words or phrases you **See**:

If you love those who love you, what benefit is that to you? For even sinners love those who love them. (Luke 6:32)

Little children, let us not love in word or talk but in deed and in truth. (1 John 3:18)

But God shows his love for us in that while we were still sinners, Christ died for us. (Romans 5:8)

Savor these truths in prayer:

> Father, today I pray that _____ would be marked by your love. You have shown us what love looks like with the greatest gift in the world, Jesus. Give them a vision of the power of Christ's love and how they can surprise and astonish the world by offering his love to others in practical ways. Cause them to love others the way that you love them, sacrificially. Give them joy in reaching out with active love that meets others right where they are. Create in them a love for others that cannot be contained. Protect them from embracing a small, selfish type of love that only loves those that love them, or the kind of love that is all talk and fake. Help them live out Jesus' love, which is authentic, true and active love that blesses all those it touches. For your glory and their good, in Jesus' name, amen.

Write down any thoughts or ideas you may want to **Share**:

Day Four: Faith

Father, open my eyes so that I might *see* you more clearly, *savor* you more fully, and *share* you more freely.

Circle or underline any key words or phrases you **See**:

Blessed is the man who trusts in the LORD, whose trust is the LORD. He is like a tree planted by water, that sends out its roots by the stream, and does not fear when heat comes, for its leaves remain green, and is not anxious in the year of the drought, for it does not cease to bear fruit. (Jeremiah 17:7,8)

Savor these truths in prayer:

> Father, thank you that you are worthy of all our trust. I pray for _____ today that they would have unwavering delight as they hope and trust in you. Make their confidence, strength, courage and tenacity in this life flow from their relentless trust in you. Cause the roots of their faith and trust to sink deep into to your faithfulness, resulting in resilient, fearless fruit in their lives because of their abiding and resting in you. Incline them to drink deeply of the truth of your word to fuel an unshakable faith and trust in your unstoppable promises. Use their lives to be a catalyst in helping countless others find their greatest joy in trusting and treasuring Christ for a lifetime. May their faith in you prompt others to live by faith in you as well. For your glory and their good, I pray in Jesus' name, amen.

Write down any thoughts or ideas you may want to **Share**:

Day Five: Purity

Father, open my eyes so that I might *see* you more clearly, *savor* you more fully, and *share* you more freely.

Circle or underline any key words or phrases you **See**:

Therefore be imitators of God, as beloved children. And walk in love, as Christ loved us and gave himself up for us, a fragrant offering and sacrifice to God. But sexual immorality and all impurity or covetousness must not even be named among you, as is proper among saints. (Ephesians 5:1-3)

Savor these truths in prayer:

> Father, thank you that we are your beloved children. Help us by the power of your Holy Spirit to intentionally reflect your character, becoming like you in love and holiness. I pray that _____ would live lives of sacrificial love like Christ did for them on the cross. Cause their selflessness to be a sweet and fragrant offering to God. Help them guard their hearts from selfishness and greed which sets the stage for sexual immorality, impurity and covetousness. Awaken their hearts and minds to see even the slightest signal of selfishness in their lives. Cause them to be quick to come to you in confession and repentance to break every link and lure of impurity. Help them to find friends that will strengthen their resolve to be faithful in becoming like you. For your glory and their good, in Jesus' name, amen.

Write down any thoughts or ideas you may want to **Share**:

Day Six: Speech

Father, open my eyes so that I might *see* you more clearly, *savor* you more fully, and *share* you more freely.

Circle or underline any key words or phrases you **See**:

The wise of heart is called discerning, and sweetness of speech increases persuasiveness. Good sense is a foundation of life to him who has it, but the instruction of fools is folly. The heart of the wise makes his speech judicious and adds persuasiveness to his lips. Gracious words are like a honeycomb, sweetness to the soul and health to the body. (Proverbs 16:21-24)

Savor these truths in prayer:

> Father, your Word says that out of the heart the mouth speaks. I pray today that _____ would have hearts that are fueled by your wisdom, love and favor so that their speech would be a fountain of sweetness and persuasiveness bringing blessings to others. Cause them to be generous in speaking gracious words that delight the heart, refresh the soul and renew the body. Help them to become wise in how to spot words that flow from either wisdom or folly. Draw them to friends whose hearts overflow with words that bring life to both soul and body and protect them from those whose words steal, kill and destroy. For your glory and their good, in Jesus' name, amen.

Write down any thoughts or ideas you may want to **Share**:

Day Seven: Conduct

Father, open my eyes so that I might *see* you more clearly, *savor* you more fully, and *share* you more freely.

Circle or underline any key words or phrases you **See**:

Thus says the LORD: "Let not the wise man boast in his wisdom, let not the mighty man boast in his might, let not the rich man boast in his riches, but let him who boasts boast in this, that he understands and knows me, that I am the LORD who practices steadfast love, justice, and righteousness in the earth. For in these things I delight, declares the LORD." (Jeremiah 9:23-24)

Savor these truths in prayer:

> Father, I thank you that you tell us that what we boast in is where we find our identity. I pray that _____ would find their identity in you and your purposes. Give them courage and diligence to resist all of the natural tendencies to find their identity in their wisdom, strength or riches. Help them know that these are good gifts from you to advance your purposes of steadfast love, justice, and righteousness on the earth. Give them confidence that every ounce of energy used to promote steadfast love, justice, and righteousness in the world brings abundant delight and joy to your heart. May their lives be a constant cause of delight to you Father. I pray this for your glory and their good, in Jesus' name, amen.

Write down any thoughts or ideas you may want to **Share**:

Notes

PRAY for ME CAMPAIGN SPOTLIGHT

The Boy with the Bell

Ed Albury was an older gentleman who had pledged to be a prayer champion for the fifth consecutive year at his church, this time for a twelve-year-old boy named Aden.

One Sunday after Ed had spoken to Aden at church, Aden turned right around and asked, "Mr. Albury, how can I pray for you?" Ed shared with Aden that he was actually battling cancer, and he asked him to pray for healing.

At the end of Ed's radiation therapy, several of his friends attended his Bell Ringing Ceremony to celebrate Ed's completion of this treatment milestone. Aden had shown up with a bell too.

When Ed saw Aden, he called him up to stand with him and shared with his friends how much Aden's prayers for him had meant and how thankful he was for their relationship through the Pray For Me Campaign.

God shaped Aden into Ed's prayer champion right when he needed it most.

PART THREE

A Week of Each Essential

Congratulations, you have just completed five weeks of praying a different Essential every day for your grandchildren. I love the variety that praying the 7 Essentials in seven days provides. However, in part three I wanted to provide you with the opportunity to focus your praying on one Essential for an entire week. I really think you will enjoy this as well. This approach will provide you with a week-long deep-dive into each Essential as you pray for your grandchildren through the lens of a specific Essential during a seven-day period.

I encourage you to remember that this Prayer Guide is designed to serve you in praying well for your grandchildren. So, if your grandchildren have specific needs that you feel you should hover over for an extended time, do it. You will probably find some prayers and Essentials that you resonate with more at different times as you go through the Prayer Guide multiple times. Be sure to mark those prayers and begin writing your own prayers that are rooted in specific passages.

Enjoy "Part Three" as your prayers bring supernatural encouragement and blessings for your grandchildren.

Week Six

Favor

To be grateful is to recognize the Love of God in everything He has given us—and He has given us everything. Every breath we draw is a gift of His Love, every moment of existence is a grace, for it brings with it immense graces from Him. — DON POSTEMA

And whatever you do, in word or deed, do everything in the name of the Lord Jesus, giving thanks to God the Father through him. (Colossians 3:17)

...pray without ceasing, give thanks in all circumstances; for this is the will of God in Christ Jesus for you. (1 Thessalonians 5:17-18)

Day One of Favor

Father, open my eyes so that I might *see* you more clearly, *savor* you more fully, and *share* you more freely.

Circle or underline any key words or phrases you **See**:

For I am the least of the apostles, unworthy to be called an apostle, because I persecuted the church of God. But by the grace of God I am what I am, and his grace toward me was not in vain. On the contrary, I worked harder than any of them, though it was not I, but the grace of God that is with me. (1 Corinthians 15:9-10)

Savor these truths in prayer:

> Father, I praise and thank you for your grace and favor. I pray that _____ would see and savor your favor for all it is worth. Let their hearts be alive and responsive to the favor of your working in their lives. Protect them from thinking that your grace is a passive thing, but cause them to see it as a mighty force that empowers them in pursuing your purposes. Guard them from believing the lie that it is in their own strength and goodness that they are making a difference in the world. Give them great delight in only boasting in you, knowing that it is by your grace that they are who they are. Create in them a relentless desire to be strengthened by your grace so that they will be tenacious in seeking to bless others for your glory and their good. In the name of Jesus, amen.

Write down any thoughts or ideas you may want to **Share**:

Day Two of Favor

Father, open my eyes so that I might *see* you more clearly, *savor* you more fully, and *share* you more freely.

Circle or underline any key words or phrases you **See**:

Satisfy us in the morning with your steadfast love, that we may rejoice and be glad all our days. (Psalm 90:14)

Savor these truths in prayer:

> Father, every day _____ will be presented with things that promise to make them happy and satisfy the longings of their hearts. You alone can satisfy their hearts and make them glad all their days. I pray that you will satisfy them early and often with your steadfast love. Protect them from believing that they would be more satisfied if they were only smarter, stronger, prettier, or richer. Give them eyes to see through the lies of these empty promises, so they can gaze relentlessly on your steadfast love all through the day. Awaken the taste buds of their hearts to savor the sweetness of your love every time they see it. Cause them to share their delight in your steadfast love freely as they live for you each day. For your glory and their good, in Jesus' all-satisfying name, amen.

Write down any thoughts or ideas you may want to **Share**:

Day Three of Favor

Father, open my eyes so that I might *see* you more clearly, *savor* you more fully, and *share* you more freely.

Circle or underline any key words or phrases you **See**:

And God is able to make all grace abound to you, so that having all sufficiency in all things at all times, you may abound in every good work. As it is written, "He has distributed freely, he has given to the poor; his righteousness endures forever." He who supplies seed to the sower and bread for food will supply and multiply your seed for sowing and increase the harvest of your righteousness.
(2 Corinthians 9:8-10)

Savor these truths in prayer:

> Father, I praise you that every aspect of your grace is available to my grandchildren. Today I pray that _____ would have unrestrained confidence in your faithful favor for them. Cause them to have unshakable trust in your ability and willingness to make all of your grace abound toward them. Remind them that your perfect and powerful supply of grace makes them sufficient in all things at all times no matter what they are facing. Awaken their hearts and minds to embrace your ongoing daily work of grace in their lives. Empower them to lean into you and your grace to fulfill your purposes in their lives. We pray this in Jesus' name, amen.

Write down any thoughts or ideas you may want to **Share**:

Day Four of Favor

Father, open my eyes so that I might *see* you more clearly, *savor* you more fully, and *share* you more freely.

Circle or underline any key words or phrases you **See**:

What then shall we say to these things? If God is for us, who can be against us? He who did not spare his own Son but gave him up for us all, how will he not also with him graciously give us all things? (Romans 8:31-32)

Savor these truths in prayer:

> Father, I pray today that _____ would sense the magnitude of your goodness for them. Let them be amazed by the fact that you are more than enough for whatever they face in this life. Let the truth that you are "FOR" them give them unstoppable courage to live for you in spite of their fears. Cause their confidence in you to be matched by a growing dependence on you, seeking the favor of your presence, protection, and provision in all of life. You have given the greatest gift of all for them in Jesus and all the resources of heaven are available to them through him. Let the significance of Jesus' life, death, and resurrection sink into the depths of their hearts. Cause their trust and treasuring of you to be fueled by the truths of Romans 8:31-32. For your glory and their good, in Jesus' name, amen.

Write down any thoughts or ideas you may want to **Share**:

Day Five of Favor

Father, open my eyes so that I might *see* you more clearly, *savor* you more fully, and *share* you more freely.

Circle or underline any key words or phrases you **See**:

Let the favor of the Lord our God be upon us, and establish the work of our hands upon us; yes, establish the work of our hands! (Psalm 90:17)

Savor these truths in prayer:

> Father, I pray for _____ today, that they would know your favor in their work. Help them to realize that they were created on purpose for a purpose. Cause them to find both joy and rest in your favor over their lives, knowing that whatever they set their hands to do can and should bring you glory. Give them clarity and confidence concerning the gifts and abilities that you have given them. Unleash your creativity over their lives to use their talents to advance your purpose in this world. In your mercy and favor, establish the work of their hands to bring blessing to others and glory to you. Give them joy in their work, and make them a joy to work with. Cause them to be intentional in pursuing your favor over their lives each day. For your glory and their good, in Jesus' name, amen.

Write down any thoughts or ideas you may want to **Share**:

Day Six of Favor

Father, open my eyes so that I might *see* you more clearly, *savor* you more fully, and *share* you more freely.

Circle or underline any key words or phrases you **See**:

Come to me, all who labor and are heavy laden, and I will give you rest. Take my yoke upon you, and learn from me, for I am gentle and lowly of heart, and you will find rest for your souls. For my yoke is easy, and my burden is light. (Matthew 11:28-30)

Savor these truths in prayer:

> Father, thank you for your great compassion and care for us. I pray today for _____ that they would hear your beautiful invitation, that everyone who is weary and weighed down with overwhelming burdens can come to you and find rest and renewal. Help them to believe this invitation is for them. Overcome any and all resistance of pride, insecurity or fear that would keep them from saying YES to your invitation of hope. Give them a vision of who you really are, gentle and lowly of heart. In your mercy, help them to humble themselves before you, rejecting self-reliance for God-reliance. Strengthen them to give themselves fully to you and your gentle care. Give them eyes to see, ears to hear and hearts to understand that your rest is perfect and will satisfy their souls. For your glory and their good, in the matchless name of Jesus, amen.

Write down any thoughts or ideas you may want to **Share**:

Day Seven of Favor

Father, open my eyes so that I might *see* you more clearly, *savor* you more fully, and *share* you more freely.

Circle or underline any key words or phrases you **See**:

He [Jesus] is the image of the invisible God, the firstborn of all creation. For by him all things were created, in heaven and on earth, visible and invisible, whether thrones or dominions or rulers or authorities—all things were created through him and for him. And he is before all things, and in him all things hold together. (Colossians 1:15-17)

Savor these truths in prayer:

> Father, thank you that Jesus is the creator and sustainer of everything, everywhere. I pray that _____ would have uncontainable joy and delight in Jesus as the source, origin, and center of all things. Cause your supremacy over their lives to create in them hope and happiness when they rise up and when they go to sleep. Remind them with the air that they breathe and the beating of their hearts that you are their perfect provider. Use their eyes, ears, taste and touch to awaken in them a deeply felt gratefulness for your provision. Cause them to be enthralled by your sovereignty in the ordinary things of life and may their delight in you never cease. In the matchless name of Jesus, amen.

Write down any thoughts or ideas you may want to **Share**:

Notes

Week Seven

Wisdom

One of the beautiful aspects of prayer is that it is not just one-directional. It is not just a cathartic experience where we unload on God to feel better. God communicates to us when we pray if we pause long enough to listen. God uses his Word and his Spirit to bring guidance, understanding, and conviction. You can be sure that he will never bring something to mind that is contrary to his Word. So ask him for guidance, understanding, and even conviction concerning anything in your world that needs to be addressed. Don't be afraid—he wants the best for you.

Search me, O God, and know my heart! Try me and know my thoughts! And see if there be any grievous way in me, and lead me in the way everlasting! (Psalm 139:23-24)

Day One of Wisdom

Father, open my eyes so that I might *see* you more clearly, *savor* you more fully, and *share* you more freely.

Circle or underline any key words or phrases you *See*:

"Blessed is the one who finds wisdom, and the one who gets understanding, for the gain from her is better than gain from silver and her profit better than gold. She is more precious than jewels, and nothing you desire can compare with her. Long life is in her right hand; in her left hand are riches and honor. Her ways are ways of pleasantness, and all her paths are peace. She is a tree of life to those who lay hold of her; those who hold her fast are called blessed." (Proverbs 3:13-18)

Savor these truths in prayer:

> Father, I pray for _____ today, that they would know the blessing of finding wisdom and understanding. Give them strong desires for you that propel them toward your truth. Awaken their spiritual taste buds to savor the fruit of a life that is focused on you and your magnificent wisdom and understanding. May they experience long life, riches, honor, and great joy as they follow your path of wisdom leading to peace and pleasantness. Cause their paths to lead to the tree of life, most specifically to the cross of Christ. It is your wisdom that made true life possible in Jesus. Cause their hearts to be relentless in pursuing your wisdom, in Jesus' name, amen.

Write down any thoughts or ideas you may want to ***Share***:

Day Two of Wisdom

Father, open my eyes so that I might *see* you more clearly, *savor* you more fully, and *share* you more freely.

Circle or underline any key words or phrases you **See**:

Let no one deceive himself. If anyone among you thinks that he is wise in this age, let him become a fool that he may become wise. For the wisdom of this world is folly with God. For it is written, "He catches the wise in their craftiness," and again, "The Lord knows the thoughts of the wise, that they are futile." So let no one boast in men. For all things are yours, whether Paul or Apollos or Cephas or the world or life or death or the present or the future—all are yours, and you are Christ's, and Christ is God's. (1 Corinthians 3:18-23)

Savor these truths in prayer:

> Father, it is so easy to be deceived into thinking that the ways of this world are wise. I pray that you would protect _____ from the deception of self-proclaimed wisdom, which is the path to foolishness. Give them a keen sense of dependence and humble confidence in you that supersedes their confidence in man. Help them see the futility of so-called wisdom that is not rooted in you. Bring loving adults into their lives who will help them drink deeply of your wisdom. Cause their hope, joy and delight to be centered in you and your wisdom. May you be their hearts' greatest boast all their days. For your glory and their good, in the name of Christ, amen.

Write down any thoughts or ideas you may want to **Share**:

Day Three of Wisdom

Father, open my eyes so that I might *see* you more clearly, *savor* you more fully, and *share* you more freely.

Circle or underline any key words or phrases you **See**:

> For I want you to know how great a struggle I have for you and for those at Laodicea and for all who have not seen me face to face, that their hearts may be encouraged, being knit together in love, to reach all the riches of full assurance of understanding and the knowledge of God's mystery, which is Christ, in whom are hidden all the treasures of wisdom and knowledge. I say this in order that no one may delude you with plausible arguments. (Colossians 2:1-4)

Savor these truths in prayer:

> Father, I long for _____ to have hearts that are full of encouragement because they are unshakably held by your love. Cause them to enjoy full assurance of knowing and understanding your mystery, which is Christ. Give them a deep understanding and joy in all the treasures of wisdom and knowledge that are hidden in Christ. May they flourish in seeing, savoring, and sharing the depths of wisdom they have found in Jesus, with their peers. Let them be so captivated by the wonder of Jesus that they would never be duped to hope in something or someone else for life and joy. Use me to show them Jesus. For your glory and their good, in Jesus' name, amen.

Write down any thoughts or ideas you may want to **Share**:

Day Four of Wisdom

Father, open my eyes so that I might *see* you more clearly, *savor* you more fully, and *share* you more freely.

Circle or underline any key words or phrases you **See**:

Walk in wisdom toward outsiders, making the best use of the time. (Colossians 4:5)

Look carefully then how you walk, not as unwise but as wise, making the best use of the time, because the days are evil. Therefore do not be foolish, but understand what the will of the Lord is. And do not get drunk with wine, for that is debauchery, but be filled with the Spirit... (Ephesians 5:15-18)

Savor these truths in prayer:

> Father, I pray today for _____, that they would walk in wisdom in all of their relationships. Cause them to understand that their choices matter and to know that every decision leads to a destination. Give them incredible delight and persistence in turning away from evil and making the best use of their time. Remind them that they were made to reflect your greatness to the world. Give them resolve to pursue righteousness every day. Your Word is the sword of the Spirit that is able to cut through the lies of this world. Give them a relentless desire to drink deeply of your Word every day. so that they will be filled with your Spirit. For your glory and their good, in Jesus' name, amen.

Write down any thoughts or ideas you may want to **Share**:

Day Five of Wisdom

Father, open my eyes so that I might *see* you more clearly, *savor* you more fully, and *share* you more freely.

Circle or underline any key words or phrases you **See**:

The Lord by wisdom founded the earth; by understanding he established the heavens; by his knowledge the deeps broke open, and the clouds drop down the dew. My son, do not lose sight of these, keep sound wisdom and discretion, and they will be life for your soul. (Proverbs 3:19-22a)

Savor these truths in prayer:

> Father, it is by your wisdom that the earth was founded and the heavens established, and for that we praise your name. I pray that _____ would see the goodness of your provision in all of creation. Cause them to learn to savor the greatness of your wisdom as they touch a blade of grass or see the stars above. May their hearts be encouraged by your sovereignty every time a raindrop splashes on their faces. Make them tenacious in seeking to enjoy the sweetness of sound wisdom and discretion in everyday life. Surround them with people who walk in wisdom and whose lives bear the fruit of your favor. For your glory and their good, in Jesus' name, amen.

Write down any thoughts or ideas you may want to ***Share***:

Day Six of Wisdom

Father, open my eyes so that I might *see* you more clearly, *savor* you more fully, and *share* you more freely.

Circle or underline any key words or phrases you **See**:

But as for you, continue in what you have learned and have firmly believed, knowing from whom you learned it and how from childhood you have been acquainted with the sacred writings, which are able to make you wise for salvation through faith in Christ Jesus. All Scripture is breathed out by God and profitable for teaching, for reproof, for correction, and for training in righteousness, that the man of God may be complete, equipped for every good work. (2 Timothy 3:14-17)

Savor these truths in prayer:

> Father, there is nothing more important than knowing you personally. Create in _____ tender hearts that are responsive to your Word so that they can become wise for salvation through faith in Christ Jesus. Don't let them be deceived by the lies of this world; assure them that Jesus is the only way by which they can be saved and made right with you. Create in them teachable hearts and minds so that they may receive the full benefits of engaging with your Word. Cause them to flourish in living in obedience to and freely sharing the truths of your Word. For your glory and their good, in Jesus' name, amen.

Write down any thoughts or ideas you may want to **Share**:

Day Seven of Wisdom

Father, open my eyes so that I might *see* you more clearly, *savor* you more fully, and *share* you more freely.

Circle or underline any key words or phrases you **See**:

Who is wise and understanding among you? By his good conduct let him show his works in the meekness of wisdom…But the wisdom from above is first pure, then peaceable, gentle, open to reason, full of mercy and good fruits, impartial and sincere. And a harvest of righteousness is sown in peace by those who make peace. (James 3:13, 17-18)

Savor these truths in prayer:

> Father, wise people bear fruit that reveals their wisdom. I pray that _____ would have a hunger and thirst for your wisdom that is clearly a gift from you. Cause them to pursue it with diligent humility, leaving behind a host of lives blessed by the fruit of the wisdom that comes from above. Give them a keen ability to spot wisdom that is from you and embrace it as their own. Cause them to bear the fruit of wisdom that is pure, peaceful, gentle, open to reason, impartial, and sincere. Bring people into their lives who know and live out your wise purposes. May their lives produce a harvest of righteousness that is sown in peace. For your glory and their good, in the precious name of Jesus, amen.

Write down any thoughts or ideas you may want to **Share**:

Notes

Week Eight

Love

Give us, O Lord, a steadfast heart, which no unworthy affection may drag downwards; give us an unconquered heart, which no tribulation can wear out; give us an upright heart, which no unworthy purpose may tempt aside. Bestow upon us also, O Lord our God, understanding to know you, diligence to seek you, wisdom to find you, and a faithfulness that may finally embrace you; through Jesus Christ our Lord. — ST. THOMAS AQUINAS

Day One of Love

Father, open my eyes so that I might *see* you more clearly, *savor* you more fully, and *share* you more freely.

Circle or underline any key words or phrases you **See**:

Love is patient and kind; love does not envy or boast; it is not arrogant or rude. It does not insist on its own way; it is not irritable or resentful; it does not rejoice at wrongdoing, but rejoices with the truth. Love bears all things, believes all things, hopes all things, endures all things. Love never ends. As for prophecies, they will pass away; as for tongues, they will cease; as for knowledge, it will pass away. (1 Corinthians 13:4-8)

Savor these truths in prayer:

> Father, your love endures forever! I pray today that _____ would receive your love through other people. Grant that they would know your patience and feel your kindness throughout this day. Give them favor to encounter people filled with your love today. Cause them to be filled with your love for others today, showing patience and kindness especially when they encounter people who are arrogant and rude. May they be the sweet aroma of Christ to people who insist on their own way. Cause your supernatural love to empower them to believe, hope, and endure all things. For your glory and their good, in Jesus' name, amen.

Write down any thoughts or ideas you may want to **Share**:

Day Two of Love

Father, open my eyes so that I might *see* you more clearly, *savor* you more fully, and *share* you more freely.

Circle or underline any key words or phrases you **See**:

A new commandment I give to you, that you love one another: just as I have loved you, you also are to love one another. By this all people will know that you are my disciples, if you have love for one another. (John 13:34-35)

Savor these truths in prayer:

> Father, I pray today for _____ that they would embrace your commandment to love one another. Give them eyes to see and hearts to understand how thoroughly you have personally loved them. Cause them to comprehend just how deep, wide, long, and high your love is for them so that they can love others fully. May they obey your command to love one another with daily diligence so that the world will know that they belong to you. Protect them from becoming casual or indifferent in how they care for others. Lead them daily by your Spirit to be agents of your love. For your glory and their good, in Jesus' name, amen.

Write down any thoughts or ideas you may want to **Share**:

Day Three of Love

Father, open my eyes so that I might *see* you more clearly, *savor* you more fully, and *share* you more freely.

Circle or underline any key words or phrases you **See**:

There is no fear in love, but perfect love casts out fear. For fear has to do with punishment, and whoever fears has not been perfected in love. We love because he first loved us. If anyone says, "I love God," and hates his brother, he is a liar; for he who does not love his brother whom he has seen cannot love God whom he has not seen. And this commandment we have from him: whoever loves God must also love his brother. (1 John 4:18-21)

Savor these truths in prayer:

Father, give _____ eyes to see their fears and grant them the confidence that your perfect love is the answer to those fears. Cause them to run to you with each and every fear so that it may be swallowed up by your perfect love. Create in them the full freedom that comes from your deep and abiding love. Help their hearts soak in your fear-killing, freedom-producing love like a brand new sponge. Where their love is weak, strengthen it. Make their hearts large in love toward you and others. Help them to learn to love others in the same way they have received love from you. For your glory and their good, in the loving name of Jesus, amen.

Write down any thoughts or ideas you may want to **Share**:

Day Four of Love

Father, open my eyes so that I might *see* you more clearly, *savor* you more fully, and *share* you more freely.

Circle or underline any key words or phrases you **See**:

> In this the love of God was made manifest among us, that God sent his only Son into the world, so that we might live through him. In this is love, not that we have loved God but that he loved us and sent his Son to be the propitiation for our sins. Beloved, if God so loved us, we also ought to love one another. (1 John 4:9-11)

Savor these truths in prayer:

> Father, thank you for making your love clear in Jesus! Cause _____ to grasp the magnitude of your love in sending your Son into the world. Help them see that their sins have separated them from you, and you solved that separation through Jesus' sacrifice. Let them savor the sweetness of your sacrifice for their sins. Cause their hearts to be filled with overflowing thankfulness because of your sacrificial love. May that love be one of the distinguishing marks of their lives. Help them love one another the way that you have loved them in Jesus. Give them eyes to see how they can show your love to others today. For your glory and their good, in Jesus' name, amen.

Write down any thoughts or ideas you may want to **Share**:

Day Five of Love

Father, open my eyes so that I might *see* you more clearly, *savor* you more fully, and *share* you more freely.

Circle or underline any key words or phrases you **See**:

For the love of Christ controls us, because we have concluded this: that one has died for all, therefore all have died; and he died for all, that those who live might no longer live for themselves but for him who for their sake died and was raised. (2 Corinthians 5:14-15)

Savor these truths in prayer:

> Father, thank you for the transforming power of Christ's love. I pray that _____ would experience the fullness of His love for them and the world. I pray that they would be controlled, compelled, and consumed by the wonder of Christ's love for them. In your mercy awaken their hearts and minds to embrace the fullness of the Love of Christ for them in his death, burial and resurrection. Saturate them in the ocean of Christ's love, so that they would no longer live for themselves, but for him and his glory and purposes. I pray this for your glory and their good, in Jesus' name, amen.

Write down any thoughts or ideas you may want to **Share**:

Day Six of Love

Father, open my eyes so that I might *see* you more clearly, *savor* you more fully, and *share* you more freely.

Circle or underline any key words or phrases you **See**:

Beloved, let us love one another, for love is from God, and whoever loves has been born of God and knows God. Anyone who does not love does not know God, because God is love. (1 John 4:7-8)

Savor these truths in prayer:

> Father, I pray for _____ that you would open their eyes to see that you are the source of all love, because you are love. Thank you that your love is like a relentless fountain that brings vibrant life to all who drink from it. Renew, replenish, and refresh them in your all-satisfying love. By your mercy, manifest through them the depth and riches of your love for the world. Keep them from ever minimizing any thought, word or deed that is not loving others. Protect them from taking lightly any tendency to hold a grudge, be bitter, or disrespectful of others. Help their lives to overflow relentless love and generosity to others. For your glory and their good, in Jesus' name, amen.

Write down any thoughts or ideas you may want to **Share**:

Day Seven of Love

Father, open my eyes so that I might *see* you more clearly, *savor* you more fully, and *share* you more freely.

Circle or underline any key words or phrases you **See**:

But I say to you who hear, Love your enemies, do good to those who hate you, bless those who curse you, pray for those who abuse you... If you love those who love you, what benefit is that to you? For even sinners love those who love them... Be merciful, even as your Father is merciful. (Luke 6:27-28, 33, 36)

Savor these truths in prayer:

> Father, thank you that your love is unlike anything the world has ever known. I prayer that _____ would taste and see that you and your love are supremely good and supernaturally powerful to transform relationships. Help them to understand that you are calling them to love in the same way that you have loved them. You have done the supreme good for all of us as your enemies by sending Jesus to die for us. Empower them to love their enemies by doing them good and praying for them. In your mercy, cause your love to soften their hearts and fill them with mercy toward others. May your name be praised because of how they love the unloving. For your glory and their good, in the matchless name of Jesus, amen.

Write down any thoughts or ideas you may want to ***Share***:

Notes

Week Nine

Faith

Praying for your grandchildren by yourself is invigorating, but I want to encourage you to consider widening your circle. Find a friend who is also a grandparent and pray together perhaps once a week. If that's too big a commitment for you, consider doing it once a month. You will find that praying this prayer guide with someone is easy and incredibly encouraging. You may find it so encouraging that you create a grandparents' prayer group to strengthen your efforts of interceding for the next generation!

For where two or three are gathered in my name, there am I among them. (Matthew 18:20)

Day One of Faith

Father, open my eyes so that I might *see* you more clearly, *savor* you more fully, and *share* you more freely.

Circle or underline any key words or phrases you **See**:

And without faith it is impossible to please him, for whoever would draw near to God must believe that he exists and that he rewards those who seek him. (Hebrews 11:6)

Savor these truths in prayer:

> Father, without faith it is impossible to please you. I pray for _____ today, that you would give them an insatiable heart that is alive with faith in your greatness as the all-satisfying King of the universe. Help them know that their faith and trust in who you are and all that you promise brings great joy and delight to your heart. Cause them to grow in their unwavering confidence that you exist and long to reward those who seek you in faith. Create in them a diligent desire to trust your promises and to seek you to bring the resources of heaven to bear on the needs of earth. Fuel their faith to trust you daily in all the highs and lows of life. Be the object of their faith and may their reward be a heart that is satisfied with all that you are for them. For your glory and their good, in Jesus' name, amen.

Write down any thoughts or ideas you may want to **share**:

Day Two of Faith

Father, open my eyes so that I might *see* you more clearly, *savor* you more fully, and *share* you more freely.

Circle or underline any key words or phrases you **See**:

Therefore, since we are surrounded by so great a cloud of witnesses, let us also lay aside every weight, and sin which clings so closely, and let us run with endurance the race that is set before us, looking to Jesus, the founder and perfecter of our faith, who for the joy that was set before him endured the cross, despising the shame, and is seated at the right hand of the throne of God. (Hebrews 12:1-2)

Savor these truths in prayer:

> Father, you have called us to a race and it is not a sprint. I ask today that _____ would run with endurance. Give them faith to overcome the discouragements and difficulties that are a part of the race. Inspire them with the lives of all those who have run in faith before them. Create in them courage to let go of the things that hold them back. Free them from their sins and empower them to forgive those who sin against them. Help them set their sights on you, Jesus, as the author and perfecter of their faith. Fill them with the same joy that empowered you to endure the cross. Cause their joy in you to strengthen, satisfy and propel them forward in faith.. May you be praised forever! In Jesus' name, amen.

Write down any thoughts or ideas you may want to **Share**:

Day Three of Faith

Father, open my eyes so that I might *see* you more clearly, *savor* you more fully, and *share* you more freely.

Circle or underline any key words or phrases you **See**:

You keep him in perfect peace whose mind is stayed on you, because he trusts in you. Trust in the LORD forever, for the LORD GOD is an everlasting rock. (Isaiah 26:3-4)

Savor these truths in prayer:

> Father, your presence is a place of perfect peace for those whose minds are focused on you. I pray that _____ would learn to fix their minds on you today with absolute trust. Give them an ever-growing confidence in you that endures through their entire lives. Establish them in your perfect peace, knowing that you are their God and their everlasting rock. Give them the ability to see fear, worry, and anxiety as signals to trust you and your promises. Cause your perfect peace to reign in their hearts. Let their faith in you give them the courage to love and care for the people you bring into their lives. Cause them to never cease to embrace you and your faithfulness as the object of their faith. May you be praised forever, in Jesus' name, amen.

Write down any thoughts or ideas you may want to **Share**:

Day Four of Faith

Father, open my eyes so that I might *see* you more clearly, *savor* you more fully, and *share* you more freely.

Circle or underline any key words or phrases you **See**:

And Jesus said to him, "'If you can!' All things are possible for one who believes." Immediately the father of the child cried out and said, "I believe; help my unbelief!" (Mark 9:23-24)

Savor these truths in prayer:

> Father, thank you for the promises that you offer in your Word. Thank you for the hope that you offer to your children who trust you with their lives. I pray that you would give _____ the ability to see and feel their personal need for you and your promises. Help them to know that feeling helpless can be one of your greatest gifts when they respond humbly by calling out to you for help. Teach them to know that all things are possible with you. Give them a daily desire to call out to you for more faith, "I believe! Help my unbelief!" Give them pleasure in trusting you in prayer. Increase their faith, for your glory and their good, in the faithful name of Jesus, amen.

Write down any thoughts or ideas you may want to **Share**:

Day Five of Faith

Father, open my eyes so that I might *see* you more clearly, *savor* you more fully, and *share* you more freely.

Circle or underline any key words or phrases you **See**:

To this end we always pray for you, that our God may make you worthy of his calling and may fulfill every resolve for good and every work of faith by his power, so that the name of our Lord Jesus may be glorified in you, and you in him, according to the grace of our God and the Lord Jesus Christ. (2 Thessalonians 1:11-12)

Savor these truths in prayer:

> Father, I echo the apostle Paul's prayer as I pray for _____ today. Empower them to lean into and live up to all that you have called them to as your children. Give them eyes of faith to see the places and situations in this world where you desire them to bring your goodness. Give them unyielding resolve to act in faith and confidence that you are giving them the strength to change the world. In your mercy and grace, may their faith and actions point others to praise, enjoy and trust in the all-satisfying name of Jesus Christ. For your glory and their good, in Jesus' name, amen.

Write down any thoughts or ideas you may want to **Share**:

Day Six of Faith

Father, open my eyes so that I might *see* you more clearly, *savor* you more fully, and *share* you more freely.

Circle or underline any key words or phrases you **See**:

Fight the good fight of the faith. Take hold of the eternal life to which you were called and about which you made the good confession in the presence of many witnesses. (1 Timothy 6:12)

I have fought the good fight, I have finished the race, I have kept the faith. Henceforth there is laid up for me the crown of righteousness… (2 Timothy 4:7-8)

Savor these truths in prayer:

> Father, I pray that _____ would learn that following you is a fight of faith to believe your good and perfect promises over the deceptive promises of the world, the flesh, and the devil. Help them surrender their hearts to you and seek the power of your Spirit to believe all that you have promised. Give them resolve to daily live by faith with a tenacious view of eternity and the life to come. Give them great joy in the truth that you have prepared a place for them as their Savior, Redeemer, and King. May the promise of eternal life with you compel them to daily fight the good fight of faith. For your glory and their good. In Jesus' name, amen.

Write down any thoughts or ideas you may want to **Share**:

Day Seven of Faith

Father, open my eyes so that I might *see* you more clearly, *savor* you more fully, and *share* you more freely.

Circle or underline any key words or phrases you **See**:

...and I pray that the sharing of your faith may become effective for the full knowledge of every good thing that is in us for the sake of Christ. (Philemon 1:6)

Savor these truths in prayer:

> Father, I pray today that _____ would fall more and more deeply in love with you. Cause their love for you to be so strong that they would freely and naturally share their faith with others. Give them joy in seeing others come to trust you alone for their salvation. Cause them to understand that sharing their faith actually deepens their hope and confidence in you and your promises. Give them the freedom to naturally share your greatness with those around them and soften the hearts of those who hear of your greatness through them. As they share, establish in their hearts the full knowledge of every good thing that is theirs because of Christ. For your glory and their good, in Jesus' name, amen.

Write down any thoughts or ideas you may want to **Share**:

Notes

Week Ten

Purity

If we don't feel strong desires for the manifestation of the glory of God, it is not because we have drunk deeply and are satisfied. It is because we have nibbled so long at the table of the world. Our soul is stuffed with small things, and there is no room for the great. — JOHN PIPER

Day One of Purity

Father, open my eyes so that I might *see* you more clearly, *savor* you more fully, and *share* you more freely.

Circle or underline any key words or phrases you **See**:

No temptation has overtaken you that is not common to man. God is faithful, and he will not let you be tempted beyond your ability, but with the temptation he will also provide the way of escape, that you may be able to endure it. (1 Corinthians 10:13)

Savor these truths in prayer:

> Father, I praise you that you are our faithful God. I pray _____ would know and experience unwavering confidence in your faithfulness in the midst of temptations. Remind them that their temptations are common and not unique to them. Protect them from the enemy of their souls who wants them to feel isolated and alone in their sin and temptations. Give them faith to believe that you will not allow them to be tempted beyond their ability. Forge in them the will and desire to staunchly resist each temptation by the power of your Spirit. For your glory and their good, in Jesus' name, amen.

Write down any thoughts or ideas you may want to **Share**:

Day Two of Purity

Father, open my eyes so that I might *see* you more clearly, *savor* you more fully, and *share* you more freely.

Circle or underline any key words or phrases you ***See***:

For this is the will of God, your sanctification: that you abstain from sexual immorality; that each one of you know how to control his body in holiness and honor, not in the passion of lust like the Gentiles who do not know God…For God has not called us for impurity, but in holiness. Therefore whoever disregards this, disregards not man but God, who gives his Holy Spirit to you. (1 Thessalonians 4:3-5, 7-8)

Savor these truths in prayer:

> Father, I praise you that your purposes and will are perfect and good. Thank you that it is your will that we would be sanctified and set apart to become like Jesus in every way. I pray that you would help _____ to pursue holiness and honor with their bodies, minds and spirits. Protect them from the lure of lust that steals, kills and destroys relationship with you and others. Create in them a passion for purity and cause them to be intentional in how they live. Help them realize the truth that to disregard your calling on their lives for purity is to disregard you personally. Cause them to have a heart for holiness that matches your heart. For your glory and their good, in Jesus' name, amen.

Write down any thoughts or ideas you may want to ***Share***:

Day Three of Purity

Father, open my eyes so that I might *see* you more clearly, *savor* you more fully, and *share* you more freely.

Circle or underline any key words or phrases you **See**:

Do not love the world or the things in the world. If anyone loves the world, the love of the Father is not in him. For all that is in the world—the desires of the flesh and the desires of the eyes and pride of life—is not from the Father but is from the world. And the world is passing away along with its desires, but whoever does the will of God abides forever. (1 John 2:15-17)

Savor these truths in prayer:

> Father, you are clear in what is good for us and what is not. Too often our appetites lead us astray. Father, I pray that you would give _____ an appetite for supreme delight and enjoyment in you. Cause their hearts and minds to be captured by your all-satisfying greatness. Guard their hearts from being enticed by the desires of the flesh, the desires of the eyes and the boastful pride of life. Grant them an acute awareness of when these earthly loves begin creeping into their hearts so they can refuse and reject them. Give them eyes to see the futility of loving the things of this world which are passing away. Cause their love for you to increase and abound in depth, breadth, length, and height so that they will delight in doing your will. For your glory and their good. In Jesus' name, amen.

Write down any thoughts or ideas you may want to **Share**:

Day Four of Purity

Father, open my eyes so that I might *see* you more clearly, *savor* you more fully, and *share* you more freely.

Circle or underline any key words or phrases you **See**:

Now to him who is able to keep you from stumbling and to present you blameless before the presence of his glory with great joy, to the only God, our Savior, through Jesus Christ our Lord, be glory, majesty, dominion, and authority, before all time and now and forever. Amen. (Jude 1:24-25)

Savor these truths in prayer:

> Father, I commit _____ to you today. You alone are able to keep them from stumbling. You alone can present them blameless in the presence of your glory with uncontainable joy. Guard them from getting sidetracked by sin and temptation. Capture their minds and hearts with the wonder of one day entering into the presence of your glory. Cause them to be diligent in moving steadily toward you and your purposes. Make them long for you and your presence. May your name be blessed and praised forever. In Jesus' name, amen.

Write down any thoughts or ideas you may want to **Share**:

Day Five of Purity

Father, open my eyes so that I might *see* you more clearly, *savor* you more fully, and *share* you more freely.

Circle or underline any key words or phrases you **See**:

Create in me a clean heart, O God, and renew a right spirit within me. Cast me not away from your presence, and take not your Holy Spirit from me. Restore to me the joy of your salvation, and uphold me with a willing spirit. (Psalm 51:10-12)

Savor these truths in prayer:

> Father, only you can create a clean heart and renew a right spirit within us. Give _____ a vision of the sweetness of being forgiven, cleansed and renewed by you. Cause them to be bothered and burdened by their disobedience to your word and will. Create in them a craving for their hearts to be free from the guilt of sin, to be cleansed and made right before you. Please protect them from becoming comfortable with unconfessed sin in their lives. Give them a longing for your presence and help them to know and respond to the Holy Spirit's leading and conviction. In your mercy, restore in them the joy of your salvation so that they may praise your great name. For your glory and their good, in Jesus' name, amen.

Write down any thoughts or ideas you may want to **Share**:

Day Six of Purity

Father, open my eyes so that I might *see* you more clearly, *savor* you more fully, and *share* you more freely.

Circle or underline any key words or phrases you **See**:

Now may the God of peace himself sanctify you completely, and may your whole spirit and soul and body be kept blameless at the coming of our Lord Jesus Christ. He who calls you is faithful; he will surely do it. Brothers, pray for us. (1 Thessalonians 5:23-25)

Savor these truths in prayer:

> Father, I praise you as the God of Peace, who sanctifies us. I pray that _____ would find great delight in being transformed into the image of Christ. In your mercy, keep their bodies, souls and spirits blameless before you. May they live their lives with a powerful sense of hope and expectation of seeing you in eternity or when you return, whichever comes first. Cause their confidence in who you are making them to be, become unshakable, so that the world would be drawn to you. Father, finish your work in each one of them. Guard them from wandering from the truth and help them surrender to your Spirit's leading each day. Fill them with your perfect and powerful peace as they pursue a life of purity. For your glory and their good, in Jesus' name, amen.

Write down any thoughts or ideas you may want to ***Share***:

Day Seven of Purity

Father, open my eyes so that I might *see* you more clearly, *savor* you more fully, and *share* you more freely.

Circle or underline any key words or phrases you **See**:

If we say we have no sin, we deceive ourselves, and the truth is not in us. If we confess our sins, he is faithful and just to forgive us our sins and to cleanse us from all unrighteousness. (1 John 1:8-9)

I acknowledged my sin to you, and I did not cover my iniquity; I said, "I will confess my transgressions to the Lord," and you forgave the iniquity of my sin. (Psalm 32:5)

Savor these truths in prayer:

> Father, I pray today for _____ to be set free from the weight and worry of personal sin. Our natural tendencies are to deny and deceive ourselves concerning the extent of our sins and failures. Give them eyes to see that denying or downplaying their sin is a deadly deception that separates them from you and others. Give them courage and confidence to confess and acknowledge their sin to you. Remind them that the freedom of forgiveness can only be felt by coming clean to you concerning their sin. Fuel their faith in your faithfulness to make them pure and holy in your sight as they live a life of confession and repentance. For your glory and their good, in Jesus' name, amen.

Write down any thoughts or ideas you may want to **Share**:

Notes

WEEK ELEVEN

Speech

One of the designs of this book is to help you make praying the Scriptures for the next generation as natural as breathing. Unlike breathing, though, identifying key passages and turning them into prayers takes a little practice. In the last chapter of this book you will have the opportunity to create your own prayers. So with that in mind, I encourage you to start taking note of any words or phrases that are especially encouraging or inspiring as you are praying. Also, be on the hunt for portions of Scripture that you would like to make the focus of your prayers. Remember to ask God for his favor while you create prayers that will bless your grandchildren.

Day One of Speech

Father, open my eyes so that I might *see* you more clearly, *savor* you more fully, and *share* you more freely.

Circle or underline any key words or phrases you **See**:

Let no corrupting talk come out of your mouths, but only such as is good for building up, as fits the occasion, that it may give grace to those who hear. (Ephesians 4:29)

Let there be no filthiness nor foolish talk nor crude joking, which are out of place, but instead let there be thanksgiving. (Ephesians 5:4)

Savor these truths in prayer:

> Father, I pray that _____ would speak life-giving words with purpose and precision. Grant that they would speak words that build up and are grace-giving to those who hear. Protect them from corrupt and foolish talk. Guard them from speech that is filled with filthiness and crude joking. Allow them to initiate conversations that are gracious and encouraging. Create in them gratefulness for all that you have done for them. I pray that thankfulness would flow freely from their lips so that you are glorified and others are uplifted. For your glory and their good, in Jesus' name, amen.

Write down any thoughts or ideas you may want to **Share**:

Day Two of Speech

Father, open my eyes so that I might *see* you more clearly, *savor* you more fully, and *share* you more freely.

Circle or underline any key words or phrases you **See**:

...do not be anxious about anything, but in everything by prayer and supplication with thanksgiving let your requests be made known to God. And the peace of God, which surpasses all understanding, will guard your hearts and your minds in Christ Jesus. (Philippians 4:6-7)

Savor these truths in prayer:

> Father, thank you that you are our hope in all circumstances. We do not need to be afraid or anxious, but when we are, we can come to you in prayer. Thank you for the gift of prayer. I pray today that _____ would diligently come to you in prayer in all circumstances. Help them know that you hear the words they speak in prayer. Cause your peace, which surpasses all understanding, to flood their hearts and minds in Christ. Help them rest in your perfect peace as it guards their hearts and minds from fear and anxiety. Cause them to pray without ceasing and make their conversations with you their most-used form of speech. For your glory and their good, in Jesus' name, amen.

Write down any thoughts or ideas you may want to **Share**:

Day Three of Speech

Father, open my eyes so that I might *see* you more clearly, *savor* you more fully, and *share* you more freely.

Circle or underline any key words or phrases you **See**:

Continue steadfastly in prayer, being watchful in it with thanksgiving. At the same time, pray also for us, that God may open to us a door for the word, to declare the mystery of Christ, on account of which I am in prison—that I may make it clear, which is how I ought to speak. (Colossians 4:2-4)

Savor these truths in prayer:

> Father, thank you that you have given us the opportunity to make your greatness known to the world. I pray that _____ would become effective in their ability to share the beauty of Christ. Cause them to deeply know and embrace your Word as truth. I pray that you would open doors for them to present truth freely and frequently. Help them to fall deeper and deeper in love with you as they read your Word. Give them clarity concerning your love and purposes for this world, and the ability to share them clearly. Give them freedom and discernment to winsomely share your truths in any setting. May they be steadfast in prayer and filled with thankfulness to tell people about you. For your glory and their good, in Jesus' name, amen.

Write down any thoughts or ideas you may want to **Share**:

Day Four of Speech

Father, open my eyes so that I might *see* you more clearly, *savor* you more fully, and *share* you more freely.

Circle or underline any key words or phrases you **See**:

Let your speech always be gracious, seasoned with salt, so that you may know how you ought to answer each person. (Colossians 4:6)

Savor these truths in prayer:

> Father, I ask today that you would fill _____ with your wisdom, love, faith, and purity. Help them to know that it is only through your grace that they can please you with their speech. Create in them speech that is gracious and seasoned with salt. Cause them to become magnets for life-giving conversations. May the words they speak be a catalyst for their hearers to hunger and thirst for you and your truth. Give them deep and abiding wisdom so that their conversations will honor your name and bless others. In the all-satisfying name of Jesus I pray, amen.

Write down any thoughts or ideas you may want to **Share**:

Day Five of Speech

Father, open my eyes so that I might *see* you more clearly, *savor* you more fully, and *share* you more freely.

Circle or underline any key words or phrases you **See**:

Have nothing to do with foolish, ignorant controversies; you know that they breed quarrels. And the Lord's servant must not be quarrelsome but kind to everyone, able to teach, patiently enduring evil, correcting his opponents with gentleness. God may perhaps grant them repentance leading to a knowledge of the truth... (2 Timothy 2:23-25)

Savor these truths in prayer:

> Father, protect _____ today from foolish speech. Give them wisdom to know when a pointless argument is emerging in conversation. Help them to have nothing to do with speech that breeds useless quarrels. Empower them to be kind and not quarrelsome. Cause them to be filled with your loving gentleness when they have to correct others. Give them patience and empathy as they graciously share about you. Remind them that quarrels divide and ruin relationships. In your mercy, grant them repentance that leads to the knowledge of your truth and restores them in relationship with you and others. May you be praised for all the gracious ways your children speak. In Jesus' name, amen.

Write down any thoughts or ideas you may want to **Share**:

Day Six of Speech

Father, open my eyes so that I might *see* you more clearly, *savor* you more fully, and *share* you more freely.

Circle or underline any key words or phrases you **See**:

Rejoice always, pray without ceasing, give thanks in all circumstances; for this is the will of God in Christ Jesus for you. (1 Thessalonians 5:16-18)
We give thanks to God always for all of you, constantly mentioning you in our prayers... (1 Thessalonians 1:2)

Savor these truths in prayer:

> Father, thank you for clearly revealing your will for us in Christ Jesus. I pray that _____ would have a lifestyle that is marked by rejoicing, prayer, and thankfulness. Cause them to find joy in your goodness each day, and help them to express that joy through praise to you. Create in them a longing to see your greatness each day, and help them express their longing in relentless prayer. Help their prayers to be saturated with thankfulness for all things in all circumstances. Give them eyes to see the good you are doing in and through others. Cause their hearts to overflow in thankfulness toward you. For your glory and their good, in Jesus' name, amen.

Write down any thoughts or ideas you may want to **Share**:

Day Seven of Speech

Father, open my eyes so that I might *see* you more clearly, *savor* you more fully, and *share* you more freely.

Circle or underline any key words or phrases you **See**:

But exhort one another every day, as long as it is called "today," that none of you may be hardened by the deceitfulness of sin. (Hebrews 3:13)

Savor these truths in prayer:

> Father, thank you that you do not let us just go our own way. Thank you that you care and correct us through your Word. Your correction is a demonstration of your great love for us. I pray that you would raise up friends for _____ who will care enough to hold them accountable. Help them to realize that loving correction is a gift that helps protect them from sin. Soften their hearts and give them eyes to see through the deceitfulness of sin. Keep them from rebelling against the people in their lives who challenge them with the truth. Grant that their hearts would be receptive and responsive to truth. For your glory and their good, in Jesus' name, amen.

Write down any thoughts or ideas you may want to **Share**:

Notes

Week Twelve

Conduct

Prayer is asking God to incarnate, to get dirty in your life. Yes, the eternal God scrubs floors. For sure we know he washes feet. So take Jesus at his word. Ask him. Tell him what you want. Get dirty. Write out your prayer requests; don't mindlessly drift through life on the American narcotic of busyness. If you try to seize the day, the day will eventually break you. Seize the corner of his garment and don't let go until he blesses you. He will reshape the day. — PAUL E. MILLER

Humble yourselves, therefore, under the mighty hand of God so that at the proper time he may exalt you, casting all your anxieties on him, because he cares for you. (1 Peter 5:6-7)

Day One of Conduct

Father, open my eyes so that I might *see* you more clearly, *savor* you more fully, and *share* you more freely.

Circle or underline any key words or phrases you **See**:

I am the vine; you are the branches. Whoever abides in me and I in him, he it is that bears much fruit, for apart from me you can do nothing. (John 15:5)

Savor these truths in prayer:

> Father, thank you for making it clear that we are dependent on you for everything. We must rely on and abide in Jesus for our spiritual life if we are to have any hope of flourishing. Apart from you we can do nothing. It is you who sustains us and empowers us each day. Cause _____ to abide in you today. Empower them by your Spirit to bear fruit that lasts. Give them a longing to rest, trust and abide in you so they can help others find their greatest satisfaction in you. For your glory and their good, in Jesus' name, amen.

Write down any thoughts or ideas you may want to **Share**:

Day Two of Conduct

Father, open my eyes so that I might *see* you more clearly, *savor* you more fully, and *share* you more freely.

Circle or underline any key words or phrases you **See**:

Therefore, since we have been justified by faith, we have peace with God through our Lord Jesus Christ. Through him we have also obtained access by faith into this grace in which we stand, and we rejoice in hope of the glory of God. Not only that, but rejoice in our sufferings, knowing that suffering produces endurance, and endurance produces character, and character produces hope, and hope does not put us to shame, because God's love has been poured into our hearts through the Holy Spirit who has been given to us. (Romans 5:1-5)

Savor these truths in prayer:

> Father, I pray that _____ would know that every challenge or trial they face has a purpose that is bigger than what they can see. Remind them that the glorious grace in which they stand is a gift from you. Help them to see glimpses of the character and hope you are forging in their lives. Cause them to see and savor the love that has been poured out into their hearts by the Holy Spirit. Strengthen them to endure suffering and may they praise you for the goodness you provide when they endure hardships. For your glory and their good, in Jesus' name, amen.

Write down any thoughts or ideas you may want to **Share**:

Day Three of Conduct

Father, open my eyes so that I might *see* you more clearly, *savor* you more fully, and *share* you more freely.

Circle or underline any key words or phrases you **See**:

His master said to him, 'Well done, good and faithful servant. You have been faithful over a little; I will set you over much. Enter into the joy of your master.' (Matthew 25:21)

For we are his workmanship, created in Christ Jesus for good works which God prepared beforehand, that we should walk in them. (Ephesians 2:10)

Savor these truths in prayer:

> Father, you have given us natural abilities and specific personalities to accomplish your purposes. I pray that _____ would long to fulfill the purposes and desires you have for them in this life. Give them a tenacity of purpose that causes them to stay the course faithfully to the end. May your supreme purpose of faithfully and fully loving you and their neighbors be their top priorities. Help them to start well in this journey of faith with you, but more importantly I pray that you would empower them to finish well. May they long to hear your wonderful words of affirmation and welcome: "Well done, good and faithful servant" and "Enter into the joy of your master." In the precious name of Jesus I pray, amen.

Write down any thoughts or ideas you may want to **Share**:

Day Four of Conduct

Father, open my eyes so that I might *see* you more clearly, *savor* you more fully, and *share* you more freely.

Circle or underline any key words or phrases you **See**:

You are the light of the world. A city set on a hill cannot be hidden. Nor do people light a lamp and put it under a basket, but on a stand, and it gives light to all in the house. In the same way, let your light shine before others, so that they may see your good works and give glory to your Father who is in heaven. (Matthew 5:14-16)

Savor these truths in prayer:

> Father, you have called us to shine in such a way that the world will know you are great. I pray that _____ would grasp the calling on their lives to shine for your glory. Don't let shyness or fear cause your light in them to be dim or hidden. Create in them courage to do works of love, kindness, mercy, and justice so that the world might be captured by your greatness. Awaken them to new ways that they can serve you and mankind that would exalt your name and goodness. Give them insight on how to help others join in the joy of serving and glorifying you through their good works. May you be praised forever, in Jesus' name, amen.

Write down any thoughts or ideas you may want to **Share**:

Day Five of Conduct

Father, open my eyes so that I might *see* you more clearly, *savor* you more fully, and *share* you more freely.

Circle or underline any key words or phrases you **See**:

Live in harmony with one another. Do not be haughty, but associate with the lowly. Never be wise in your own sight. Repay no one evil for evil, but give thought to do what is honorable in the sight of all. If possible, so far as it depends on you, live peaceably with all. (Romans 12:16-18)

Savor these truths in prayer:

> Father, your call on our lives is personal and practical. Thank you for the admonitions in this passage that show us how to live a flourishing life with others. I pray that _____ would find joy in pursuing a life of harmony with others. Do not let them think more highly of themselves than they should. Help them to resist having a proud spirit. Empower them to naturally engage with those who are less fortunate than they are, knowing that everything they have is by your gracious hand. Never let them desire revenge for wrongs suffered. Give them the power of your spirit to do what is honorable in the sight of all, just as Jesus did when he unjustly suffered. Create in them a passionate desire to live at peace with everyone. For your glory and their good, in Jesus' name, amen.

Write down any thoughts or ideas you may want to **Share**:

Day Six of Conduct

Father, open my eyes so that I might *see* you more clearly, *savor* you more fully, and *share* you more freely.

Circle or underline any key words or phrases you **See**:

So whether you eat or drink, or whatever you do, do all to the glory of God. (1 Corinthians 10:31)

And whatever you do, in word or deed, do everything in the name of the Lord Jesus, giving thanks to God the Father through him. (Colossians 3:17)

Savor these truths in prayer:

> Father, thank you that our lives belong to you. You created us by your power and for your glory. It is only when we live for your glory that our lives can be fulfilled. I pray that you would draw _____ to yourself today so they would know the sweetness and power of your presence. Give them strength, desire, and passion to do everything they do today for your glory. Help them to give thanks to you in all things. Cause them to enjoy each moment of their life, knowing that it is a gift from you. Make their heart overflow with thankfulness to you in all they say and do, reminding them that you are the provider of all things. May your name be exalted by whatever they do today. For your glory and their good, in Jesus' name, amen.

Write down any thoughts or ideas you may want to **Share**:

Day Seven of Conduct

Father, open my eyes so that I might *see* you more clearly, *savor* you more fully, and *share* you more freely.

Circle or underline any key words or phrases you **See**:

But exhort one another every day, as long as it is called "today," that none of you may be hardened by the deceitfulness of sin. (Hebrews 3:13)

Savor these truths in prayer:

> Father, I pray today that _____ would have a keen personal awareness concerning the sins and temptations to which they are most susceptible. Protect them from these presumptuous sins. Help them have a healthy fear for these sins that can dominate their lives. Give them resilience in guarding their hearts and minds from loving and lingering near these sins. In your mercy and lovingkindness use the challenges and trials that they face to break the hold of rebellion in their lives. Draw their hearts toward the power of your word. Help them memorize, meditate and muse over the truths of your word and cause it to transform their daily thoughts, words and deeds. For your glory and their good, in Jesus' name, amen.

Write down any thoughts or ideas you may want to **Share**:

Notes

PRAY for ME CAMPAIGN SPOTLIGHT

Prayer Meets Milestones

A young man named Will participated in the Pray for Me Campaign at his church. He was 18 years old, had no father figure, and had yet to learn to drive.

Will's prayer champion Steven found this out through forming a relationship with him, and he took the opportunity to teach Will to drive.

What started with prayer led Steven to become the resource that met a need for Will, modeling the body of Christ as it was designed.

When Steven committed to the Pray for Me Campaign, God used his relationship with Will to meet Will's spiritual needs as well as practical.

PART FOUR

Giving Blessings

Dave and Kim Butts

In the course of preparing this book I was in Orlando, Florida for a gathering of prayer and next-generation leaders. I had the honor of sitting down for an interview with Dave and Kim Butts who have four grandkids. Dave serves as the chairman for America's National Prayer Committee. In our time together they shared how they had been giving blessings to their youngest son since he was about two years old. The power of receiving a blessing came home to both Dave and Kim when their son, on the eve of his wedding, came into their room and knelt beside their bed and asked to receive a blessing one more time. After a lifetime of receiving a blessing he wanted to feel the goodness of it one more time as he entered this new stage of life. It was a powerful moment. Both Dave and Kim now continue blessing their grandchildren the way they did their children.

What if some of the most dominant memories your grandchildren have of you were the times when you gave them blessings? When they were sitting in your lap, or just before bedtime as you sat on the edge of their bed. Perhaps it was on a key birthday or another significant moment in their lives when you spoke a God-saturated blessing over them. What if in each of these moments they remember you placing your hand gently on their head or shoulder while you lovingly looked deep into their eyes saying:

"The LORD bless you and keep you [their name here]; The LORD make his face to shine upon you and be gracious to you; The LORD lift up his countenance upon you and give you peace." Along with this blessing they remember you speaking additional blessings rooted in God's word, specifically designed for that occasion, to inspire and encourage them in what God wants to do in and through them.

This can happen and it is happening for young people around the world by parents, grandparents and other significant adults who understand the biblical goodness of giving blessings to the next generation. As God intended, it is life changing for everyone involved when his people speak blessings over his people.

It should not be surprising that the idea and implementation of giving blessings originates with our heavenly Father. To receive the blessing of God is one way to receive the favor of God to flourish in some way. We can see this pattern from the earliest recorded blessings in the Bible:

> *So God created man in his own image, in the image of God he created him; male and female he created them.* ***And God blessed them****. And God said to them, "Be fruitful and multiply and fill the earth and subdue it, and have dominion over the fish of the sea and over the birds of the heavens and over every living thing that moves on the earth."* (Genesis 1:27-28)
>
> ***And God blessed Noah*** *and his sons and said to them, "Be fruitful and multiply and fill the earth..."* (Genesis 9:1)
>
> (Speaking to Abram who became Abraham) "...***I will bless those who bless you****, and him who dishonors you I will*

*curse, **and in you all the families of the earth shall be blessed.**"* (Genesis 12:3)

The Bible is full of passages that reveal God's intention to show his people favor and to help them flourish. This is one clear type of blessing in the Bible. In his book "The Family Blessing", Rolf Garborg says there are actually four types of blessing found in Scripture: First, there is the blessing spoken by God to people, like those listed above. Second, there is the blessing spoken by people to God, like the beginning of Psalm 103. Third, there is the blessing spoken by God or people over things, like Jesus praying over food. And Fourth, there is the blessing spoken by one person to another, like Numbers 6:24-27. All of these are important, but for our purposes we will focus on the blessings spoken by one person to another. Garborg explains that this fourth type of blessing has a general sense and a specific sense. Each of us has hopefully experienced a blessing in the general sense. This is where someone speaks well of, affirms or expresses praise for you in some way. Think about when this has happened to you. Perhaps your parent, spouse or friend spoke encouragement into your life. You probably didn't identify it as a "blessing" then, even though now, when you think about it, you definitely remember feeling blessed at the time. These blessings are appropriate and powerful and should be a regular part of how we engage with our children and grandchildren. They should feel exceptionally blessed when they are with us.

According to Garborg, "The more specific meaning of blessing is the intentional act of speaking God's favor and power into someone's life, often accompanied by a gesture such as laying hands on the person." One of the most famous of all the blessings recorded in the Bible is found in Numbers 6:24-27. This particular blessing was the official blessing that the Lord commanded Moses to have Aaron and the priests say over the people of Israel:

> *"'...The LORD bless you and keep you; The LORD make his face to shine upon you and be gracious to you; The LORD lift up his countenance upon you and give you peace.' So shall they put my name upon the people of Israel, and I will bless them."*

Imagine you are Aaron and his team of priests. This blessing was a command of God and speaking this blessing over the people of Israel was not optional for them. It was a core part of their job description. God intended this blessing and the fruit of it to be a primary source of bringing his goodness and favor to his people. I love the culminating verse, verse 27, that immediately follows these three statements of blessing. This verse gives us the behind-the-scenes intention of God in commanding this blessing to be pronounced over the nation of Israel: "So shall they put my name upon the people of Israel, and I will bless them." *Wow!* Slow down and let this soak in. When God commanded the priests to proclaim this blessing over the people of Israel, he was actually placing his all-encompassing name upon them. This is really a big deal. God himself is doing something powerful through the priests when they pronounce this blessing over his people.

I think at this moment it is important to realize that God in his mercy has made us, his people who are united with Christ, a royal priesthood. It's true! Theologians call this royal priesthood "The priesthood of all believers". Of course, there is a lot of goodness that flows through the truth of the priesthood of all believers, but here is one implication concerning giving blessings: each of us, as followers of Christ, can and should look for appropriate opportunities to speak words of blessing over others. As parents and grandparents we have a specific responsibility to pronounce and speak blessings over our children and grandchildren. When we embrace this simple act of obedience, we can trust that God is working supernaturally through us to actually bring his blessing on our children and grandchildren. It is simply amazing that God has established you to speak the riches of his goodness over your grandchildren by giving them blessings.

It may be important here to note that giving blessings is similar to prayer, in that it is an incredibly powerful spiritual activity, and yet prayer and blessings are slightly different. The difference rests in the audience for each. In prayer, God is the one we are speaking to concerning our praise, thanksgiving or petitions. When giving blessings we are speaking to our children or grandchildren as the conduit of God's blessing to them. That's what Aaron and the priests did for the people of Israel and it is what we can do for our children and grandchildren.

Giving blessings may be a new or foreign idea for you right now, but stay with me and in the next few pages I will share why it is such a treasured part of my parenting even with my adult children and why it can be for grandchildren as well. I will try to give you a taste of the goodness that comes from God through the act of "giving a blessing" as experienced in my own life.

Our Journey of Giving Blessings

It was 1993 and my wife was living large, literally, as a petite woman who was pregnant with twin girls. I remember those days well as my bride spent over half of the pregnancy on bed rest because of premature contractions. Like most soon-to-be parents, we were doing everything we knew to prepare to be the best parents we could. In the process of our preparation, we came across two books that helped shape our understanding of the importance of giving blessings to your children and by God's grace, to your grandchildren. The first book was Gary Smalley and John Trent's classic book on the subject called *The Blessing*. I had read it back in my seminary days, but now it was taking on a whole new significance. This book was foundational in sparking my desire to bless our daughters and grandchildren, whenever they came along. However, it was Rolf Garborg's book, *The Family Blessing,* that actually sealed the deal concerning this parental provision for my bride and me. In his book, Garborg shares about the biblical practice of giving blessings along with his own personal story.

As I look back on those early days as a parent, I had a lot of unspoken uncertainty, which was intermingled with my growing sense of joy in the approaching arrival of our daughters. As a newbie parent, who by God's grace had tasted and seen some of his goodness personally, I was determined to help my daughters have access to the sweetness of seeing, savoring, and sharing the greatness of Jesus Christ from the earliest stages of their lives. There was so much that I felt unprepared for as a parent, so my approach was to find and focus on a few vital actions that would influence the rest of my parenting. Basically, I needed some clear, powerful principles that I could implement daily that had the potential of lavishing wave upon wave of God's goodness on my daughters.

In *The Family Blessing*, Garborg speaks of how he and his wife would give blessings to their children every day from their earliest days as children. Here is where the idea of giving blessings took hold of my heart and has never let go: Garborg says that even as his children moved into their late teens they would come to him and his wife to receive their blessings each night. Even when they were away from home, they would call home to receive their blessings. As someone who has been involved in full-time vocational youth ministry, it did not take much for me to know in my heart that I wanted that kind of spiritual bond with my daughters, beginning at their birth. Thus my wife and I decided that giving blessings would be a core part of our parenting plan. Now, after giving blessings for more than a quarter of a century I would not hesitate to say that it can be one of the most important bonding, nurturing, and soul-strengthening things that can be done for both children and grandchildren.

Early Beginnings

In our family, the blessings we prayed over our daughters had the tendency to take on the flavor of the specific life stage they were in at the time. When our daughters were babies, we would sing their blessings to them. Michael Card had a "Lullaby" album that had the words to the Numbers 6:24-26 blessing put to music. This song made it easy to hold them and gently sing these words of blessing over them. Admittedly, it was more soothing when my wife sang to them, but they still seemed to be comforted when I blessed them in this way.

As they became a little older, we would place our hand on their heads and alternate between singing and speaking the blessing over them as they lay in their beds. Gradually, we transitioned to just speaking the blessing over them with our hand resting on their heads.

"No, no daddy, look at me!"

Parenting toddlers always provides for excitement, surprise, and sometimes some treasured insight. I remember one time when I was giving my daughter, Bethany, her blessing and I closed my eyes and began the blessing. I had only said a few words when I heard her say, "No, no daddy, look at me!" She wanted to see me look at her as I spoke the blessing over her. She was my teacher that night on how to upgrade the benefit of giving a blessing. Up to that point I might have my eyes open or closed with no real rhyme or reason, but not after that. My daughter taught me the importance of intentional eye contact.

During the elementary ages of our girls we would spend time as a family reading missionary biographies from a series by Youth With A Mission or YWAM for short. These were incredible times when we would be temporarily transported to India with Ida Scudder, the great medical missionary, or to Africa with Mary Slessor of Calabar. My wife and I had made a commitment to have a family time of devotions with our girls in a way that suited their age. When they were younger we used a resource from Desiring God for children (now called Truth:78) that had key stories from the Old and New Testaments with a corresponding coloring book. I would read the story and they would color the picture and tell us about the story. As they got older we shifted to the missionary biographies. When they entered middle and high school we tended to read a chapter from the proverbs or another book of the Bible, alternating with great Christian books. Our family devotions together had a powerful influence on the content of the blessing I spoke over my daughters each evening. For example, if we were reading about Mary Slessor of Calabar, in family devotions, I would probably give a blessing that reflected that.

The Lord bless you and keep you, Abby and Bethany. The LORD make his face shine upon you and give you peace. May the LORD give you courage, compassion, and tenacious faith like Mary Slessor of Calabar. In the name of the Father, Son, and Holy Spirit. Amen.

My goal was for my daughters to not only be inspired by the lives of these great missionaries, but also to sense that God has his hand on their lives as well. I have also found that it's important to make the blessing personal. It doesn't take much to do so, but it does make a difference. You can always add more to the ending of the blessing depending on the needs of the child you are blessing at that moment. But remember, asking for God's blessing is no small thing. Having the security, favor, and peace of God flowing toward you is foundational to life!

Coming Full Circle

It's been over a quarter of a century since God inspired my wife and me with Rolf Garborg's book, *The Family Blessing*. In that time, my daughters have received over 12,000 blessings each (and that is being conservative!). As children they would receive blessings from both parents daily and twice a day during the early elementary years of school; once as they went off to school and another as they went to bed each evening. I am thankful that there is no such thing as receiving too many blessings. This simple parenting act has truly proved to be more of a blessing to our whole family than I ever imagined.

When my daughters were about three years old we were visiting my dad and stepmother. We always enjoyed visiting them over the years. My dad loved our daughters and enjoyed having them around. On this particular trip my daughter Abby decided in her take-charge, three-year-old way that Paw Paw and Granny Ann should join us for our family devotions. Abby was unaware that they did not embrace our hope in Jesus but was able to persuade them to join us. They didn't know that joining us meant that they would also be given prayer requests to pray for as well. God was gracious in using a grandchild to open the way to share the sweetness of knowing Jesus in our devotional time. The night was concluded by Abby approaching my father to give him a blessing. My dad was sitting on a bar stool when she came to do her deed. I remember my dad turning to me with a puzzled look on his face, asking me what Abby wanted. I told him that I thought she wanted to give him a blessing and that all he needed to do was lean over and she would take care of the rest. That moment is still clear in my mind with my dad leaning over and his three-year-old granddaughter reaching up and placing her hand on his head, gently uttering the words, "The LORD bless you and keep you and make his face shine upon you and give you peace. In the name of the Father, Son, and Holy Spirit. Amen." I never imagined that incorporating giving blessings to my daughters would have blessed my unbelieving father. The blessings of God's grace always seem to spill over onto others.

For my daughters' junior years of college, they had to travel to school for the beginning of the semester at different times, because one of them had to report early for her Resident Assistant (RA) responsibilities. When you translate that, it means I had the opportunity to make the 12-hour round trip to their college two times in a two-week period. On my second journey I had successfully delivered my non-RA daughter to school and was readying myself for the 6-hour trek home. I had made my rounds, saying goodbye, and was about to leave when one of my daughters called out for me to wait as she came up to the car. What happened next confirmed to me that giving blessings to my children is the most powerful parenting tool ever invented by our heavenly Father. She looked at me through the open car door window, and proceeded to reach in through the window placing her hand on my head and gave me a blessing. The goodness of the family blessing had come full circle in that moment. That brief but lingering moment immediately entered my top ten list of greatest parenting moments! I hope and pray that these few pages have convinced you to make giving your children or grandchildren blessings a key strategy for nurturing them spiritually, emotionally, and relationally.

So, How Does it Work?

Giving blessings to your grandchildren is both simple and profound all at the same time. As we saw from Numbers 6:24-27, the blessing can be spoken over a group by a spiritual authority. Pastors in many churches do this every week at the end of a worship service. On a personal level, when you are blessing an individual child, it is an intentional moment of simply speaking God's truth over them as you lift them to the Lord.

What you say and how you go about the process of giving your grandchildren blessings can vary, but be confident that the benefits for your grandchildren in receiving blessings will endure. As I think about the aspects that are involved in giving a biblical blessing to my daughters, I have taken my cues from some of the patriarchs in the Old Testament and from Jesus in the gospels. Here is a beautiful example of Jacob (or Israel) as a grandparent giving blessings to Joseph's sons in Genesis 48:9-10:

Joseph said to his father, "They are my sons, whom God has given me here." And he said, "Bring them to me, please, that I may bless them." Now the eyes of Israel were dim with age, so that he could not see. So Joseph brought them near him, and he kissed them and embraced them.

Giving blessings is a close personal experience. Jacob wanted his grandsons close to him and when they came close "he kissed them and embraced them." Giving blessings is an overflow of your love and care for the children you are blessing.

> *And Israel stretched out his right hand and laid it on the head of Ephraim, who was the younger, and his left hand on the head of Manasseh, crossing his hands (for Manasseh was the firstborn).* (Genesis 48:14)

Jacob placed his hands on their heads and then pronounced a blessing that was specific to these two boys. You can give the same blessing to every child like the Numbers 6 blessing and make simple changes that will be specific and special to each individual child you are blessing. This is much like how I would adjust my blessing for my daughters based on what may have been happening in their lives that day.

> *And he blessed Joseph and said, "The God before whom my fathers Abraham and Isaac walked, the God who has been my shepherd all my life long to this day, the angel who has redeemed me from all evil, bless the boys; and in them let my name be carried on, and the name of my fathers Abraham and Isaac; and let them grow into a multitude in the midst of the earth."* (Genesis 48:15-16)

Then in the New Testament Jesus shows us how it is done even in a culture where children were commonly undervalued.

> *…And they were bringing children to him that he might touch them, and the disciples rebuked them. But when Jesus saw it, he was indignant and said to them, "Let the children come to me; do not hinder them, for to such belongs the kingdom of God. Truly, I say to you, whoever does not receive the kingdom of God like a child shall not enter it." And he took them in his arms and blessed them, laying his hands on them.* (Mark 10:13-16)

I love how Jesus engages with children. He takes them into his arms, giving them hugs, and laying his hands on them, he blesses them. As you can see it is a very simple and straightforward gift to a child. I like what Rob Rienow says in his book, *Visionary Parenting*: "When parents regularly speak blessings to their children it increases their sense of peace and safety." The same is true of grandparents.

John Piper said in an "Ask Pastor John" episode referring to the Mark 10 passage, "It's a very Christlike thing to do: to bless children, laying our hands on our children as we speak a blessing over them."

What if my grandkids are older?

What if my grandkids are already in elementary, middle or high school? Is it too late to start? Absolutely not! It is never too late to start lavishing your grandchildren with blessings. You will just need to do a little groundwork because this will most likely be new for your grandchildren. It is very important to understand your context and setting as you seek to introduce giving and receiving blessings to your grandchildren.

Don't be afraid to start small. Depending on your relationship with your older grandchildren, it may be best to start by just saying "The Lord Bless you [their name]" as you hug them goodbye. It may work best to introduce the idea as something you have recently come across in a book you were reading and were encouraged by an idea you wanted to begin implementing into your family. Try not to surprise them. You want them to feel as comfortable with the process as possible. Let them know what you are thinking so they will know what to expect and begin to enjoy the process. Tell them it is like a prayer but it is different because you will actually be speaking God's blessing over them. Again, depending on your relationship, you will place your hand on their head or possibly their shoulder and look them in the eye and say the blessing. You may even start out by reading the blessing from Numbers 6 as your starting point. Ultimately you will want to memorize the blessing so that it will feel more natural. Enjoy the journey.

Autumn Gold Gleanings

I love the phrase "Autumn Gold". It just rolls off the tongue. "Autumn Gold" is a phrase I coined referring to the insights and stories that I learn from sage believers in their senior years. These saints are in the Autumn season of their lives and their insights and stories are so valuable it's like collecting gold, thus the phrase "Autumn Gold". Many times what these seasoned saints have to share is absolutely priceless, but "Autumn Priceless" just doesn't have the same ring to it.

Each of us has a story and as followers of Christ our stories reflect our response to God's working in and through our lives. The greatest spiritual legacies that you read or hear about tend to be linked to individuals, families, churches and ministries that have responded in faith and obedience to God's working in their lives. For most of us, the latter stage of our lives, the autumn season, begins to bring what truly matters into vivid focus especially as it relates to our grandchildren. This is why over the last couple of years I have spent time interviewing, surveying, and speaking with hundreds of grandparents. In this section I hope to give a glimpse into the Autumn Gold Gleanings I gathered from those interviews and surveys.

In these interviews and surveys, I have sought to explore some of the challenges and dreams these grandparents have for and with their grandchildren. I often found myself on holy ground while I listened to grace-filled God stories from these grandparents. As I have reflected on these stories and conversations, I have found some significant themes that have emerged. My goal in this section is to highlight these themes while providing some quotes and brief commentary from what I have learned.

Before we launch into these Autumn Gold Gleanings, I wanted to share a fun fact that emerged over the course of my grandparent interviews. Of those I was privileged to interview, two emerged as front-runners in the most grandchildren and great grandchildren category. These grandparents are actually dear friends. They live just a few miles from each other and have attended the same church for many years. At the time of writing, the top spot belonged to Hugh and Nancy Maclellan with twenty-two. As the leaders they are edging out Frank and Dottie Brock who are holding steady at twenty-one grandchildren. However, in my conversation with Frank and Dottie, Frank light-heartedly wanted me to know that even though Hugh was leading with overall grandchildren, he was leading in the per capita standing since he only has three children and Hugh has four. He also humbly pointed out that they are definitely winning in the great grandchildren category with five in contrast to Hugh's three.

When I quote someone from an interview, I will put the quote below his or her name. It is my hope that these gleanings will prove to be encouraging and enlightening for you in your grandparenting journey. Please remember that the information that follows is not exhaustive. These ideas, insights and encouragements are an echo of what many grandparents think and feel. Enjoy the journey.

Know the Importance of Your Relationships

I thought I would start off by stating the obvious. Being a grandparent is all about relationships. Your title "Grandparent" is a relational title. It declares who you are in relation to your children's children. As obvious as that is, it doesn't necessarily mean that these relationships will be easy. Relationships can be beautiful and satisfying gifts from God and yet they can also be challenging and extremely messy. Ultimately, the themes that follow speak into how we can better navigate the relationships that God has given us. Unfortunately, we've not arrived. We are all growing in our ability to nurture and mend fractured relationships. Though the causes of relational rifts are countless, the processes for restoring the relationships tend to be pretty straightforward, but not easy. Developing healthy relationships requires skill, tact, love, kindness, humility, honesty, confession, repentance and forgiveness. As Christian grandparents you need to take the initiative in restoring, renewing and nurturing your relationships. These efforts will be part of how you will bless the generations to come.

Barry St. Clair

"Relationships are everything – When our kids were distant geographically and sometimes emotionally, we needed to have this picture in our minds. You are the father of the prodigal son, so to speak. You go to the edge of your border and put your toes on the line and spread your arms way out. Your kids need to know that you are here with your arms open."

David and Jane Neall

"Our chief goal is to maintain a relationship. If this is lost, we lose our influence."

"Be a safe person."

"Let humility and honesty guide you!

Be intentional about revisiting history with your children, asking: Where did I hurt you? Where do you feel I need to fix things between us? Asking them to forgive you and admitting you did things wrong."

"I would love to know that my kids would sense being delighted in and loved."

"Do they feel accepted, seen, and loved?"

"Create a foundation of respect and honor: Asking for permission to speak into their lives. Never give parents unsolicited advice."

"Lead with Love!"

Joe Novenson

"Grandparents ought to be the biggest, fastest, deepest repenters their grandkids have ever seen. According to Matthew 18, the greatest in the kingdom are the biggest, fastest, repenters around. Grandkids need to see this and unfortunately this is the last thing that they are seeing."

Jan Harrison

"What I've had the most experience in is reminding people that God is bigger than our mistakes. He longs for people to know him and love him. Yes, you may have been asleep at the switch when you raised your children but now you know. Because now you know you can trust him and sow into these children."

Jane Henegar

"It all starts by loving and encouraging (not directing) your children as they parent."

Knowing what You Know Now, How Would You Encourage Other Grandparents

Most of the grandparents that I had the privilege to interview were veterans in this role. I smile as I remember each of these interviews. I was amazed by a strong sense of humility with each grandparent. It was so refreshing. As I'm sure you have experienced, humble people are delightful to be around. So as you read each of these thoughts below, please know that the origin of each is humility.

Frank Brock

"Be the kind of grandparent that you wish you had had! Be intentional."

"Don't be in competition. Not just with your children or the in-laws, but even your friends."

Rodger and Suzanne Piersant

"Seek to be as authentic as you possibly can about your love for Jesus, your kids and your grandkids. It is a daily process of working it out. When you mess up, demonstrate how to apologize and ask for forgiveness. Love and prayer, we can't see how to make it through without those two."

Jan Harrison

"Don't lose a minute. Time is short. It's wake up time. It won't be long before they are 14,15, 16. They grow up fast. Nothing is more important than your family and knowing Jesus."

Scotty Smith

"Cultivate the skill of curiosity or as Jack Miller would do so often: Show the gift of Intrigue."

"Give your grandkids a sense that you are glad to see them. Giving them a sense of "Welcome" makes the gospel more believable."

Barb Novenson

"For the most part, parents are doing the best that they can. So, it isn't the best strategy to constantly be in correction mode, because that typically will not get the best response back and in effect distances you from your grandchildren. You have to be your children's support network as well, with listening and prayer."

Linda and Pete Austin III

"We love all our grandchildren very much and want them to know that we love them. We seek to treat all the grandchildren the same. Our goals have been to help them love the Lord and each other."

Jane Henegar

"If you choose to be a grumpy or critical grandparent, you are not going to get many visits. Grandparents are to celebrate the promise they see in their grandchildren. In the process of becoming who God made them to be, little ones do need our prayers. They are works in process—but so are their grandparents. For that reason we have needed, and sought, our grandchildren's prayers for us."

Kathleen Buswell Nielson

"We want to encourage our grandchildren to love and serve the Lord with all their beings! I suppose that's the overall goal that shapes all the others."

"In the end, as grandparents who are closer and closer to meeting the risen Christ face to face, we want to play a part in helping our grandchildren be ready to meet him, too."

Bob and Barbara Holt

"As grandparents we need to be flexible with our expectations and at each stage of life we need to be a little more flexible with our expectations."

Paul Miller

"Enjoy them!"

Remember to Stay in Your Lane

It is clear with all of the interviews and surveys that becoming a grandparent is one of the most exciting seasons of a person's life. Unfortunately, sometimes our enthusiasm gets the best of us and we lose our sense of propriety. Usually when this happens, some boundary ends up getting unintentionally crossed. It's easy for this to happen when your children have children. We tend to reason that we have certain rights and privileges since we are their grandparents. Well, as we all know, these little cherubs are first your children's children, which means they are driving how these new relationships will transpire. As much as we have loved to be in charge when it has come to our own children, we are not in charge of how this new season will go. This is a difficult lesson a lot of grandparents are learning the hard way. Hopefully these thoughts will provide some guardrails to help you stay in your lane.

Frank and Dottie Brock

"We told our kids when they got married that we were not going to give them advice unless they ask us for it. We would not wait for them to ask our advice if it was a matter of life or death, or quality of life issue."

"We never wanted to outdo our children concerning our grandchildren for Christmas or birthdays."

Joe and Barb Novenson

"Ask permission. Don't assume you can do anything you want with your grandchildren."

Crawford Loritts

"Don't compete with your children. They are the parents. Be their ally. Never ever, ever show their parents up in front of their kids. Honor the rules and regulations their parents have put in place. Be careful of trespassing boundaries."

Barry St. Clair

"At times we have implemented what we call the 'Horse Whisperer' approach to Grandparenting. We stand in the middle of the ring and be quiet. Not inviting ourselves into anything our children are not inviting us into. Or we are not going to give advice where they are not asking. If we wait here long enough there is going to be time when they start inviting us to be a part of things."

Linda and Pete Austin III

"Don't be helicopter grandparents."

"Your grandchildren belong first to their parents, not to you."

Genuinely and Graciously Invest in Your Grandchildren's Faith

The number one hope and desire of Christian grandparents from the survey we conducted was for their grandchildren to know and love Christ.* Relationship with Christ is the defining relationship both for this life and the one to come. May each of us seek to genuinely and graciously help our grandchildren to trust and treasure Christ more than anything else. (* See appendix)

Crawford Loritts

"Keep pointing them to the scriptures in a natural, relational way like Deuteronomy 6. We find out what they are going through and encourage them to seek the Lord about those things, even the little ones. I think there is an intersection between your heart and what is important to you with their lives. But it has to be done in an authentic way. It has to be real. Sometimes there is a fear-based thing that hits us because we are scared they are going to get in trouble and we start preaching to them. Don't get me wrong, warnings are important. I think when they see the unconditional love you have for them and the reality of your walk and your seeking to be the model of the destination for them…they are just drawn more to that reality."

"It's so important to tell them stories. Stories of God's supernatural intervention!"

"Always seek to be helping them to "own their faith." We may be their grandparents, but God doesn't have grandchildren."

"At appropriate times reminding them that no one can walk with God for them, but them. Driving them toward internalization, toward making the transition from beliefs to convictions. Which means that you have to put them in situations where they may fail. You can only have convictions when your beliefs are tested."

Dave and Kim Butts

"Giving blessings to your children and grandchildren even before they are born." (See the Giving Blessings chapter)

Jan Harrison

"The best thing we could ever do for our grandkids is to raise our own children to love Jesus. The most powerful thing we can do as parents and grandparents is to lead them to Jesus."

Kathleen Buswell Nielson

1.) We pray with and for them.

2.) We try to show them by our lives that we love God's people, the church—going to church regularly and joyfully, caring for those who need help, participating with enthusiasm in the life of a local church congregation, and encouraging the children to do so as well. Of course, grandparents are not the ones in charge, and we must respect the responsibility of the parents in these matters.

3.) We regularly read and talk about God's Word, the Bible—not just in church or for church, but in our daily lives and in the midst of our comings and goings (cf. Deuteronomy 6:4-9).

4.) We often play Christian songs. They love the Getty family albums.

5.) In the end, they see our lives and hear our words. We strive to show Jesus to them. We often fail. When we fail, we aim to admit it and ask for forgiveness.

Joe Novenson

"Narrate their lives through the lens of the Gospel. When communicating with our grandchildren we are seeking to narrate their lives and what we are seeing in them with the gospel. For example: When they excel in something, I write them and say to them, 'that is a gift God's giving you and I can't wait to see what that will be like as you spread your wings.'"

Bob and Barbara Holt:

"We seek to remind each of our grandchildren that God's made them for a purpose to use their gifts and abilities to bless others."

Be Available and Accessible as Much as You Can

Life has a plethora of limitations and grandparents feel these challenges in a real and personal way. The top two challenges that emerged from our grandparent survey were distance from grandchildren and limited time with them. These challenges require grandparents to do things that, in the not so distant past, we never would have imagined doing, i.e. Zoom calls, facetime, Skype, etc. Relationships tend to grow the best when they are in proximity; however, when distance prohibits this we must create a different kind of proximity. Do your best to be creative in being available and accessible.

Crawford Loritts

"The whole idea is "presence" even if you can't be there physically. Communicate with the parents, scheduling time to be with them. FaceTime, write notes, phone calls."

Dave and Kim Butts

"Connect as often as possible and be as accessible as possible to your grandchildren. Let them know that they can call or text any time."

Jan Harrison

"You have to be very intentional to be PRESENT. Know what they like and their weaknesses so you can PRAY into that and talk to them about that."

"It's a big deal to be present. Go to their ball games. You have to schedule. I think our older two grandchildren who are 12 and 9 now are getting a sense that they have a tribe around them with their grandparents, aunts, and cousins. They know they are cared for. Our daughters know that we are there for them, not to tell them what to do but to support them."

(I love the idea of building a "tribe" around our grandchildren. This is essentially what the Pray for Me Campaign is doing for young people in churches around the country.)

Joe and Barb Novenson

"We seek to be alert to needs and opportunities where we can be helpful for our kids and grandchildren, which means we will make sacrifices for these relationships. When each of our grandchildren were born Barb would go for 6 weeks at a time to help in any way that was needed."

The commitment to "being there" took on a special meaning when I heard the story of Joe and Barb's first grandson's birth. Here is the setting: Joe and Barb live in Chattanooga, TN and their oldest son was in seminary in St. Louis where their first grandchild, Hans, was born on a Friday morning. Friday night, Joe and Barb had to attend their daughter's high school play and Sunday morning Joe was scheduled to preach. Undaunted, Barb's mother, who lived with them, was eager to meet her first great-grandchild immediately, so they seized their one-day window of opportunity. Driving 6 hours there, spending 6 hours holding baby Hans and taking pictures, and then driving 6 hours home to Chattanooga, made a great memory.

Paul Miller

"When it comes to loving your grandchildren, it's hard to love without presence, not presents. You get quality of time in quantity of time."

Use Your Gifts and Interests to Connect with Your Grandchildren

God has given each of us gifts, abilities, and interests. These are some of the resources at our disposal when we are seeking to connect with our grandchildren. In this section I provide a sampling of some of the gifts I gleaned from the grandparents I interviewed. The key is to apply Jane Henegar's wisdom: "Find the gifts the Lord has given you and pursue that with your grandchildren." With that in mind, I encourage you to take an inventory of some of your gifts and interests after you finish this section. Explore how you can use them to make some memories with your grandchildren!

John Atherton has written a series of 3 children's books for his grandchildren. Actually, these books grew out of John's noticing his five- and eight-year-old grandchildren's imagination. He spent time storyboarding with them and that provided the genesis of the first book which he wrote based on their collaboration. He used the same process for the following two books.

Dottie Brock uses her creative artistic gifts to teach her grands how to knit, quilt, write in calligraphy, garden and make paper with dried flowers they would pick.

Frank Brock Using his woodworking gifts, he would love to involve grandchildren in projects he was working on that would help others: Like building a bridge and hiking trail from their neighborhood to Covenant College; a "Rest Stop"- a shady spot for Thrive Assisted Living residents; a "Potting Shed" for the community garden in their neighborhood; He would also do new projects his grandchildren wanted to create, like making furniture using their drawing plans.

Jane Henegar uses her gift of calligraphy to write scripture cards for every day of each grandchild's first year of college.

Henry Henegar uses the means of writing notes and letters to express his encouragement and affirmation of his grandchildren throughout the year. He also writes prayers of blessing for each of his grandchildren for their birthdays and other milestones in their lives.

Scotty Smith takes his grandkids fishing. He loves it, they love it and, in the process, he is helping to narrate the Gospel into their times together as they enjoy God's creation.

Joe Novenson teaches them how to whittle when they turn nine and gives them a penknife that their parents hold onto until they feel their children are ready to have it.

Joe is also a master storyteller and writer and he uses these gifts to create stories for both his grandsons and granddaughters. In these stories Joe will seek to bring Christian truths alive in a natural and winsome way. For his grandsons he has created an imaginary story of a man named Merrill. Merrill is an 82-year-old archeologist who is built like Arnold Schwarzenegger at his peak and looks like Sean Connery in the movie Medicine Man with a long ponytail. Merrill never ages, he is always 82. In the stories Merrill takes the boys on archeological digs all over the world. Most of the time when the boys are away Joe will send them letters from Merrill that he types and signs with his left hand. He then takes the letter outside and burns the edges and rubs them in the dirt, saying, as Merrill, "I'm writing you from Nepal. There has been an earthquake and I've come to help the Christians dig people out." (This is just a taste of the adventures of Merrill.)

Joe also wrote a lullaby for their first granddaughter that a friend put to music.

Barb Novenson uses her gift of hospitality to turn their basement into grandchildren central with their dad and uncle Andrew's toys. In the hallway leading to the basement they have all the pennants from all the schools where their parents and uncle have taught, creating a living history. Barb is also a master back scratcher who gladly provides her services for each grandchild before bed.

Mark and Judy Heinemann combine their skills to connect

with their grandchildren through loving hospitality, tutoring, storytelling and baking. They are a great team.

Chuck and JoAnne Zeiser are also a great team. Chuck is a

gifted craftsman who uses his skills to help his grandchildren learn how to fix and build things. JoAnne uses her gifts in making things to create treats and savory foods that her grandchildren love to eat.

Peggy Michaels has five grandchildren and is a retired physical

education teacher who has multiple sclerosis. She may be one of the most joyful, welcoming people I have ever met and her grandchildren are the happy recipients of her encouragement and kindness. Even with her limitations she told me in our interview, "As long as I can go, I'm going. I'm going to be with them. Going to their games and activities." She has an open-door policy with her grandchildren and their friends, which sets the stage for ongoing connection. While I was interviewing her at her home one of her grandchildren popped in with a friend looking for batteries and something to drink.

Make Some Memories that Your Grandchildren will Treasure

Every encounter with our grandchildren is a moment that can make a memory or at least will feed their memories of us. I remember hearing a couple of truisms when I was in graduate school. The first goes like this: "People don't care how much you know until they know how much you care." The second was a similar phrase: "People may forget what you say, but they will never forget how you made them feel." To make those sayings more pertinent to our conversation just replace the word "people" with "grandchildren." Your grandchildren are poised and ready for memories of joy and kindness from you. As Scotty Smith said so clearly in my interview with him: "Give your grandkids a sense that you are glad to see them. Giving them a sense of 'Welcome' makes the gospel more believable." Remember, every moment can make a memory.

Kathleen Buswell Nielson

"But I'd say, too, that along with all the special occasions that we might call milestones, there are the ordinary days and events: the meal shared, the sleepover when everybody cuddled in Grandma and Grandpa's bed, the books read, the cookies we baked and decorated together. At this point we're making *little* milestones! And the little ones are very good."

Crawford Loritts

"When our grandsons turn 13 I give them the Bible I have studied, preached and taught from. I also give them our family crest."

Dave and Kim Butts

"We pray blessings over them on their birthdays and intentionally invite mentors to be there for their 18th birthday to pray blessings over them as well."

Barry St. Clair

"I took my grandson on a Papa "Retrace Trip", retracing key places in my life and sharing how God met me along the way in those places."

Frank and Dottie Brock

"At age 12 we take each of our grandchildren on a trip for a week. Each grandchild gets their own trip. It is an opportunity to affirm where they are and get to know them in a deeper way."

Linda and Pete Austin III

"Birthdays: We have made birthdays special times of celebrating. Every time there is a birthday, we have a gathering for them in town. If they are out of town, we have gone to them to celebrate. When there is more than one birthday in a month, we will celebrate the whole group at once."

"Mission Trips: We have taken the grandchildren in small groups on mission trips."

"Family Trips: We sought to take them on family trips that would be fun, educational and spiritual. We would have a theme verse that we would memorize together and we would have devotions each night as a family. When grandchildren were old enough, they would lead the devotions."

Paul Miller

"I have Grandpa Camp for my grandchildren. When we can't be together, we take tours on FaceTime. It's cheap fun that we do together when we aren't able to actually be together. I'm always hunting for things I can do with them. One time I went "Dumpster Diving" for cardboard boxes to create a pirate ship that ended up looking more like a tanker than a pirate ship. I want to help them cultivate delight and imagination."

Joe and Barb Novenson

"When our grandkids get to a certain age we take each of them away for a few days. It can be to the city or country. On this trip we give them a really good backpack, a really good study Bible and a letter from us that says that this is everything we want you to know about Christ for their age level."

The Role of Prayer in Your Grandparenting

Every time I sat with a grandparent to do an Autumn Gold interview I was amazed, encouraged, and extremely hopeful because of the emphasis they put on prayer. Prayer plays a primary role for each of these grandparents as they seek to invest in the lives of their grandchildren. They are embracing prayer as one of the great gifts of God to us, his people, to join him in bringing about his purposes in the world. They know that prayer gives every Christian grandparent a powerful and loving way of bringing their grandchildren before the throne of grace, helping them taste and see that the Lord is good. Enjoy some of their thoughts below.

Dottie Brock

"You know what it takes to raise children and grandchildren. Who more should be the best ally, prayer warrior for your children and grandchildren than you the grandparent?"

Joe and Barb Novensen

"Prayer is 'essential, every day.' Ask parents for concrete information."

Joe sends the grandchildren the prayers that he is praying for them.

Scotty Smith

"Nothing is more daily for my wife and I than praying for our kids and grandkids."

"There is no greater gift, no greater declaration of dependence and affirmation of God's faithfulness than to pray."

"We want to use our time with our grandchildren prayerfully and really demonstrate the welcoming heart of the Gospel that we are praying into their experience."

Dave and Kim Butts

"Everyone's situation is different but one thing every grandparent can do is pray into that child's life and ultimately that is the best thing you can do."

Barry St. Clair

"Every morning we get on our knees and pray for two families a day."

"Two prayers: Pursue Jesus with all their heart, soul and mind and that they would live under God's protection, Ps. 91:11."

"We seek to pray for them in their presence."

Linda and Pete Austin III

"Both in our personal devotions and then together after breakfast each day, we pray for every grandchild and family member. We like receiving their prayer request and using these requests in our prayers for them."

Linda uses brightly colored 3x5 index cards. When she is with each grandchild, she has him or her write down his or her prayer requests on the card. So, the actual requests are written in the grandchildren's handwriting. This process gives a window into their lives because they share what is really on their hearts.

Pete chooses one book of the Bible each year and after reading it through a number of times, finds seven verses from that book to pray each day of the week for each of his grandchildren and family members. (See appendix for example)

Jane Henegar

"Prayer is a Christian grandparent's primary role and the legacy that far outlasts your final breath. That's the place to lay out any concerns, trusting the One who is listening and will answer."

Henry Henegar

"Write out your prayers for your grandchildren and send them to them. Also, pray the values you want them to embrace, like faithfulness and generosity."

Rodger and Suzanne Piersant

"The core of our grandparenting is praying for our grandchildren."

Kathleen Buswell Nielson

"Prayer is central. Perhaps because we grandparents are not the ones in charge, we learn better to pray, as we cannot direct and control in the same way we often aimed to do as parents. We pray for our *children* as they parent—how they need us to pray for them! They surely need our prayers much more than our critiques. And for our grandchildren, we have perhaps more time to pray than we did particularly as young parents. We might know the Scriptures better, so that we can choose verses to pray for them—maybe a special verse for each grandchild each year, and certainly ongoing prayers that grow out of our regular Bible reading. For a grandchild who is fearful about something, we might come on Hebrews 13:6 and pray that this child by God's grace might learn to say confidently: 'The Lord is my helper; I will not fear; what can man do to me?'"

"We grandparents sometimes tend to fear for our grandchildren, sensing that the world is changing fast and not always for the good ... What kind of a world will they grow up to live in? Prayer allows us to trust God and his good redemptive purposes in this world, through Jesus Christ his Son. Prayer allows us to commit our grandchildren into God's good hands, asking him to shape them and use them as lights in a world that needs light."

"Perhaps this is the most important thing we can do as grandparents—call out to God, both for ourselves and for the generations to follow."

Paul Miller

"My love begins in prayer for my grandchildren."

"I have very big access to them in prayer."

"Watching and praying go hand in hand, we see areas of need and we pray".

"Part of my praying is dreaming for them."

Some Brief Thoughts on Establishing a Godly Heritage or Legacy

Leaving a legacy or establishing a godly heritage is really about how your life will be remembered. It's about the ongoing impact of your life (see the introduction). Every godly heritage or legacy will at least be touched by, and most likely saturated by, the sweetness of the fruit of the Spirit. You know those nine qualities in Galatians 5 that the Holy Spirit produces in us: Love, joy, peace, patience, goodness, kindness, gentleness, faithfulness and self-control. May each of our lives produce the fruit of the Spirit so steadily and clearly that the fragrant aroma of Christ will dominate the memory of our lives.

Scotty Smith

"I would love to think, at my funeral what would come to mind for those who speak, was that he loved well to the end. He got more kind and gentle the older he got, more present and playful. So, I think the legacy of getting a healthier legacy of gospel astonishment, that as we get older Jesus is more beautiful to us. And our kids will see that rather than just telling them, 'You got to really make sure you love God', our life actually shows what it looks like to fall more deeply in love with God."

"It is what we treasure and cherish that will be what will most affect our kids and grandkids. They see what we are giving our lives to."

Jane Henegar

"The real legacy is your stories, your values, your prayers and your love. That is your legacy."

Crawford Loritts

"Leaving a legacy gets back to the eloquence of modeling. The Bible is incarnational. All leadership is incarnational in the Bible. It's not that we are perfect. Leadership is prophetic, meaning you have to be a portrait of that desired destination. That's the price you have to pay. I think the important thing is being what you want them to become, in an authentic way, and allowing them to catch that from you without necessarily sermonizing so much. It is the reality of your life."

"The first words that my grandchildren ever heard me say to them is the Loritts family verse, Joshua 1:8:

This Book of the Law shall not depart from your mouth, but you shall meditate on it day and night, so that you may be careful to do according to all that is written in it. For then you will make your way prosperous, and then you will have good success.

"The word of God is everything."

"The only thing that is permanent is God himself and what he wants to do. I think when you realize that; it creates a little bit of a sense of urgency about how you live and what you are pointing them to. Be careful of over-orchestrating their lives, but always be pointing them back to that God has a plan for you. He has a signature over your soul. You were born for something. I think if they see you living that out and talking about that, it captures their imagination and their hearts."

Paul Miller

"Pray and Love with the goal of building faith."

A Story of how God can use a Grandchild to Influence a Grandparent

A Life Chosen that Eternally Changed Another

In my grandparent interview with Hugh Maclellan, he shared the story of how he and his wife's youngest daughter Elizabeth came into the world and the unexpected impact she had on their family.

His wife Nancy had had a procedure to prevent them from having any more children. However, Nancy regretted the decision and had the procedure reversed. Soon after, she was pregnant at the age of 43.

Nancy's parents were not Christians at the time. When her father heard the news, he urged Nancy to have an abortion out of love and concern for her. However, when Nancy and Hugh's daughter Elizabeth entered the world, she began to melt her grandfather's heart as Hugh recalls.

Elizabeth and Nancy's dad would spend time together playing pool and other games as she grew and by the age of 4 or 5, Hugh declares this little girl had won her grandfather over. A bright man, he began to look into the Bible, examining it closely and, this time, understanding it from a new lens.

Nancy's dad accepted Christ at 80 years of age, professing his testimony to the elders, and joining the Church. Elizabeth, the child this man had wanted aborted, led him to truth and salvation in Christ at the end of his life.

The space between 4 years old and 80 years old seems quite the chasm. But for Elizabeth and this lost man, it was simply the length from one end of a pool table to the other, the short path a child's open heart travelled to touch that of her closed off grandfather.

When Nancy chose life for her child, little did she know God would use that little life to ultimately bring eternal life and flourishing to her own father's aged body and soul.

Today, Elizabeth is the mother of five of Hugh and Nancy's twenty-two grandchildren.

Pray for Me Campaign Spotlight

Prayer Meets Milestones Part Two

Zach was a student who almost had to leave college because he could not afford it.

One of his prayer champions from his home church stayed in touch and checked in to see how his first semester had been. Zach shared he would not be able to afford continuing school.

That prayer champion then appealed to other prayer champions in the church who eventually found and provided the resources not only to fund Zach's second semester but the rest of his college career as well.

When Zach's three prayer champions committed to pray for a high school student, they probably couldn't fathom the scope of impact it would have on Zach. But they trusted God, who was faithful to use their relationships through the Pray for Me Campaign to change the trajectory of Zach's life.

PART FIVE

Praying for Their Salvation

No one enters this life a follower of Christ. If we are God's children it is because we were born spiritually sometime after we were born physically. I like how Crawford Loritts says it: "We have grandchildren but God only has children." Your grandchildren need to have their own personal relationship with God through Christ. God uses our prayers as one of the means of drawing people to himself. We all know this and, in this section, I want to focus on how you can pray intentionally for your grandchildren's salvation. I love the zing of clarity that John Piper shares in his book about missions, *Let the Nations Be Glad*:

> *Missions is not the ultimate goal of the church. Worship is. Missions exists because worship doesn't. Worship is ultimate, not missions, because God is ultimate, not man. When this age is over, and the countless millions of the redeemed fall on their faces before the throne of God, missions will be no more. It is a temporary necessity. But worship abides forever.*

Wow! Piper uses the term "missions," but he could have just as easily said "evangelism"—the principle is the same. Missions or evangelism is not the ultimate goal, but it is a means to helping as many people as we can to join us in what we were created for. We pray and share the Gospel with those who don't know Christ so that they can enjoy the unceasing pleasure of worshipping his magnificence for eternity. So how can you pray in a way that will help your grandchildren see and savor the beauty of Jesus personally?

Three Starter Strategies for Praying for Your Grandchildren's Salvation

Strategy One: Know the Gospel

A great place to start is making sure you understand the key components of the Gospel and beginning to pray through each one of these components for your grandchildren. There are lots of great resources available to help you understand the Gospel more fully and share it with your grandchildren. Two that I want to specifically recommend are Everystudent.com and Dare 2 Share. Everystudent.com's motto is "A Safe Place to Explore Questions About Life and God" and it serves as just that. Dare 2 Share, a ministry that equips students to share their faith, has a wealth of great resources on their website (www.dare2share.org) and mobile apps, which are incredibly helpful in understanding and sharing the Gospel. Their Life in 6 Words G.O.S.P.E.L. approach has helped me and countless others gain understanding in the straightforward message of the Gospel. Lastly, Greg Stier, president of Dare 2 Share, has written a 40-day devotional that is very helpful in understanding the Gospel more fully. Take a minute to read over the Life in 6 Words G.O.S.P.E.L. listed next:

- **G**OD created us to be with Him.
- **O**UR sins separate us from God.
- **S**INS cannot be removed by good deeds.
- **PA**YING the price for sin, Jesus died and rose again.
- **E**VERYONE who trusts in Him alone has eternal life.
- **L**IFE with Jesus starts now and lasts forever.[1]

I encourage you to hover over each aspect of the G.O.S.P.E.L. Let each truth sink deeply into your heart and mind so that you feel the weight of it: the God who created you to be with him; the tragedy of how your sin separates us from God; the hopelessness of trying to be good enough to remove your sin; the amazing love and sacrifice of Jesus who paid the price for our sin by his death and resurrection; the inexpressible joy that all who trust in Jesus for salvation have eternal life; the unwavering hope that life with Jesus starts the moment you place your trust in him and never ends. Memorize this acrostic and begin to pray through it for your grandchildren so that they would know and embrace the Gospel.

Strategy Two: Prepare the Soil

The Bible is a story of redemption from the first pages of Genesis to the end of Revelation. God gives us behind-the-scenes sneak peeks throughout the Bible into how he redeems people and draws them to himself. The five passages starting on the next page are some that I've come across over the years that are instrumental in how I pray for those who do not yet have a relationship with Jesus Christ. This is definitely not a complete list of passages you could pray to prepare the way for your grandchildren to trust Christ, but

I think it will help you get started. Feel free to add to them and create your own more extensive list, as you pray for your grandchildren and others in your life who don't know Christ.

Strategy Three: Pray The 7 Essentials with a Salvation Slant

This third strategy is simple. Use the entire Prayer Guide as an effective daily tool in praying for those in your world who don't know Christ. The prayers are already deeply rooted in the Gospel and our need for Christ in all things, so praying through The 7 Essentials for your grandchildren who don't know Christ will only require you to adjust your thinking a little. Praying for your grandchildren's salvation is one of the most important things you can do for them. It is amazing that God chooses to use your prayers as one of the means of helping your grandchildren come to know him personally.

[1] ©Dare 2 Share. www.dare2share.org. Used by permission.

PREPARING THE SOIL: PRAYING FOR YOUR GRANDCHILDREN TO KNOW CHRIST

Becoming a follower of Christ is the single greatest thing that can ever happen to anyone at any time. It is a great privilege to plead with God to do his work: drawing people to himself and making them alive by shining the light of the greatness of Christ in their hearts as referenced below in 2 Corinthians 4:4-6. May God be pleased to use your prayers and lives to bring your grandchildren to himself.

In their case the god of this world has blinded the minds of the unbelievers, to keep them from seeing the light of the gospel of the glory of Christ, who is the image of God. For what we proclaim is not ourselves. But Jesus Christ as Lord, with ourselves as your servants for Jesus' sake. For God, who said, "Let light shine out of darkness," has shone in our hearts to give the light of the knowledge of the glory of God in the face of Jesus Christ (2 Corinthians 4:4-6).

No one can come to me unless the Father who sent me draws him. And I will raise him up on the last day (John 6:44).

Day One: Give Them Eyes to See

Father, open my eyes that I might *see* you more clearly, *savor* you more fully, and *share* you more freely.

Circle or underline any key words or phrases you **See**:

In their case the god of this world has blinded the minds of the unbelievers, to keep them from seeing the light of the gospel of the glory of Christ, who is the image of God. For what we proclaim is not ourselves, but Jesus Christ as Lord, with ourselves as your servants for Jesus' sake. For God, who said, "Let light shine out of darkness," has shone in our hearts to give the light of the knowledge of the glory of God in the face of Jesus Christ. (2 Corinthians 4:4-6)

Savor these truths in prayer:

> Father, I ask that you would thwart the efforts of the god of this world to blind _____ from your greatness. Remove the blinders from their minds and give them the ability to see the full light of the Gospel of Christ. Shine in their hearts the knowledge of the glory of God through the face of Jesus Christ. Cause all of their senses to be saturated by the wonders of Jesus Christ so they would turn to him for eternal life. Cause their hearts and minds to find enormous delight in every new thing they learn about your greatness. For your glory and their good, in Jesus name, amen.

Write down any thoughts you may want to **Share**:

Day Two: Draw Them

Father, open my eyes that I might *see* you more clearly, *savor* you more fully, and *share* you more freely.

Circle or underline any key words or phrases you **See**:

No one can come to me unless the Father who sent me draws him. And I will raise him up on the last day. It is written in the Prophets, 'And they will all be taught by God.' Everyone who has heard and learned from the Father comes to me... Truly, truly, I say to you, whoever believes has eternal life." (John 6:44-45, 47)

Savor these truths in prayer:

> Father, draw _____ to yourself. Be the all-powerful magnetic force that pulls them into relationship with you. Cause them to desire more out of this life than what they can see. Create in them a desire for a relationship with you. Teach my friends truth in their hearts. Give them ears to hear and understand what you want them to know so they will believe and have eternal life. May these prayers be used to draw them to yourself. For your glory and their good, in Jesus' name, amen.

Write down any thoughts you may want to **Share**:

Day Three: Make Them Alive

Father, open my eyes so that I might *see* you more clearly, *savor* you more fully, and *share* you more freely.

Circle or underline any key words or phrases you **See**:

And you were dead in the trespasses and sins...But God, being rich in mercy, because of the great love with which he loved us, even when we were dead in our trespasses, made us alive together with Christ—by grace you have been saved... (Ephesians 2:1, 4-5)

Savor these truths in prayer:

> Father, I pray for _____ who are spiritually dead. They need you to make them alive. In your abundant mercy make them alive with Christ. I pray you will break the hold of spiritual death and give them life by your matchless grace. There is no hope apart from your grace that moves in and brings to life the spiritually dead. Use your Word and Spirit to awaken them. You are the only one who can give them life and yet you use people like me to share your Word and to plead their case before your throne. Empower me to stay the course in caring for my grandchildren through prayer and actions. For your glory and their good, in Jesus' name, amen.

Write down any thoughts or ideas you may want to **Share**:

Day Four: Give Them the Gift of Faith

Father, open my eyes so that I might *see* you more clearly, *savor* you more fully, and *share* you more freely.

Circle or underline any key words or phrases you **See**:

For by grace you have been saved through faith. And this is not your own doing; it is the gift of God, not a result of works, so that no one may boast. (Ephesians 2:8-9)

So faith comes from hearing, and hearing through the word of Christ. (Romans 10:17)

And without faith it is impossible to please him, for whoever would draw near to God must believe that he exists and that he rewards those who seek him. (Hebrews 11:6)

Savor these truths in prayer:

> Father, _____ need an outpouring of your lavish grace so that they can be saved through faith. Give them faith to believe that there isn't anything better than knowing Jesus Christ personally. Help them realize they're lost without you, and that without faith they have no hope of pleasing you. Give them ears to hear the truth from your word about Christ, believing in him with all their hearts and minds. Help them to know that their relationship with you is not based on their performance, but on you giving your Son to die for our sins. Remove all the obstacles to their believing so they can be in relationship with you forever. In Jesus' name, amen.

Write down any thoughts or ideas you may want to **Share**:

Day Five: Purity

Father, open my eyes so that I might *see* you more clearly, *savor* you more fully, and *share* you more freely.

Circle or underline any key words or phrases you **See**:

Or do you presume on the riches of his kindness and forbearance and patience, not knowing that God's kindness is meant to lead you to repentance?" (Romans 2:4)

Savor these truths in prayer:

> Father, you are so good and glorious in all that you do. The riches of your kindness and patience are lavished on us every day of our lives, and yet we are often blind to your gifts. I pray you will give _____ eyes to see your kindness toward them today. As you help them see the magnitude of your kindness and patience, I pray you would soften their hearts toward you. Cause your kindness to have its way in their hearts so they would repent and turn away from trying to find true life outside of you. Help them turn away from fleeting pleasures that can never satisfy and turn towards your Son, who came that they might have life in abundance. For your glory and their good, in Jesus' name, amen.

Write down any thoughts or ideas you may want to **Share**:

WEEK THIRTEEN

Praying the Proverbs

Praying the Scriptures is an exhilarating exercise that God can use to expand your heart and mind for him. As you are praying for your grandchildren, you will find that you may need to pray about some very practical applications of The 7 Essentials. This is where I want to encourage you to pray the Proverbs. God has given us an entire book of succinct truths that bring clarity to the practical aspects of life in the Proverbs. Fresh, vibrant, real-life issues are made crisp and clear by the wisest man to step foot on earth—not including Jesus, of course. There are thirty-one chapters, so you could pray through a chapter a day if you choose. Or, you could take your time and pray through a chapter over the course of a week. For this week, I am going to take chapter three of Proverbs and demonstrate how to pray through it. Praying through the Proverbs will eventually cover each of The 7 Essentials as you work through the thirty-one chapters. May God be praised!

Day One

Father, open my eyes so that I might *see* you more clearly, *savor* you more fully, and *share* you more freely.

Circle or underline any key words or phrases you **See**:

My son, do not forget my teaching, but let your heart keep my commandments, for length of days and years of life and peace they will add to you. Let not steadfast love and faithfulness forsake you; bind them around your neck; write them on the tablet of your heart. So you will find favor and good success in the sight of God and man. (Proverbs 3:1-4)

Savor these truths in prayer:

> Father, I pray for _____ today, that you would keep their memories fresh and clear with the truths of your Word. Cause them to embrace your commands as daily guidance, resulting in long and peace-filled lives. Help them to take hold of your steadfast love and faithfulness and keep it in the forefront of their minds. May they create written reminders throughout their lives of your love and faithfulness. Show them how these have provided them favor and good success with you and man. For your glory and their good, in Jesus' name, amen.

Write down any thoughts or ideas you may want to **Share**:

Day Two

Father, open my eyes so that I might *see* you more clearly, *savor* you more fully, and *share* you more freely.

Circle or underline any key words or phrases you **See**:

Trust in the LORD with all your heart, and do not lean on your own understanding. In all your ways acknowledge him, and he will make straight your paths. Be not wise in your own eyes; fear the LORD, and turn away from evil. It will be healing to your flesh and refreshment to your bones. (Proverbs 3:5-8)

Savor these truths in prayer:

> Father, thank you for your promises. Cause _____ to have complete and unwavering trust in you and your promises today. Keep them from leaning on their own understanding which is limited and faulty. Give them the ability to see and acknowledge your working in their lives each day and trust that you will make their paths clear. Guard them against being wise in their own eyes. Cause them to fear you and turn away from even the hint of evil. Don't let them get comfortable with or delight in the slightest evil thing. Create in them a longing for holiness and righteousness that exalts you and your goodness. May you bring a wave of healing and refreshment to their bodies that would point the world to your greatness. For your glory and their good, in Jesus' name, amen.

Write down any thoughts or ideas you may want to **Share**:

Day Three

Father, open my eyes so that I might *see* you more clearly, *savor* you more fully, and *share* you more freely.

Circle or underline any key words or phrases you **See**:

Honor the LORD with your wealth and with the firstfruits of all your produce; then your barns will be filled with plenty, and your vats will be bursting with wine. My son, do not despise the LORD's discipline or be weary of his reproof, for the LORD reproves him whom he loves, as a father the son in whom he delights. (Proverbs 3:9-12)

Savor these truths in prayer:

> Father, I praise you as the provider of all things. I pray for _____, that you would enlarge their hearts for you today. Give them uncontainable pleasure in honoring you with the wealth that you have provided. Help them to know that their hope lies in you, not how much money they have in the bank. Your promises are true and you have made it clear throughout your Word that you will take care of them, as they trust you. Remind them that any season of discipline they receive from you is a sign of your absolute love for them. For your glory and their good, in Jesus' name, amen.

Write down any thoughts or ideas you may want to **Share**:

Day Four

Father, open my eyes so that I might *see* you more clearly, *savor* you more fully, and *share* you more freely.

Circle or underline any key words or phrases you **See**:

Blessed is the one who finds wisdom, and the one who gets understanding, for the gain from her is better than gain from silver and her profit better than gold. She is more precious than jewels, and nothing you desire can compare with her. Long life is in her right hand; in her left hand are riches and honor. Her ways are ways of pleasantness, and all her paths are peace. She is a tree of life to those who lay hold of her; those who hold her fast are called blessed. (Proverbs 3:13-18)

Savor these truths in prayer:

> Father, I pray for _____ today, that they would know the blessing of finding wisdom and understanding. Give them strong desires for you that propel them toward seeking wisdom and understanding. Let them taste the treasures of a life that is marked by your magnificent wisdom and understanding. May long life, riches, and honor be theirs, along with great joy as they follow your path of wisdom leading to peace and pleasantness. Cause their paths to lead to the tree of life, most specifically to the cross of Christ. It was your wisdom that made life possible in Jesus. Cause their hearts to pursue your wisdom above all else. In Jesus' name, amen.

Write down any thoughts or ideas you may want to **Share**:

Day Five

Father, open my eyes so that I might *see* you more clearly, *savor* you more fully, and *share* you more freely.

Circle or underline any key words or phrases you **See**:

The LORD by wisdom founded the earth; by understanding he established the heavens; by his knowledge the deeps broke open, and the clouds drop down the dew. My son, do not lose sight of these—keep sound wisdom and discretion, and they will be life for your soul and adornment for your neck. Then you will walk on your way securely, and your foot will not stumble. If you lie down, you will not be afraid; when you lie down, your sleep will be sweet. (Proverbs 3:19-24)

Savor these truths in prayer:

> Father, it is by your wisdom that the earth was founded and the heavens established, and for that we praise your name. I pray that _____ would see your provision in all of creation and savor the greatness of your wisdom in every blade of grass and every star above. May their hearts be encouraged by your sovereignty every time a raindrop splashes on their face. Make them tenacious in not losing sight of the preciousness of sound wisdom and discretion in everyday life. May they taste the fruit of wisdom and discretion deep within their souls. Give them security, stability, peace, and sweetness of sleep because of it. For your glory and their good, in Jesus' name, amen.

Write down any thoughts or ideas you may want to **Share**:

Day Six

Father, open my eyes so that I might *see* you more clearly, *savor* you more fully, and *share* you more freely.

Circle or underline any key words or phrases you **See**:

Do not be afraid of sudden terror or of the ruin of the wicked, when it comes, for the LORD will be your confidence and will keep your foot from being caught. Do not withhold good from those to whom it is due, when it is in your power to do it. Do not say to your neighbor, "Go, and come again, tomorrow I will give it"—when you have it with you. (Proverbs 3:25-28)

Savor these truths in prayer:

> Father, I pray for _____ today, that they would not be fearful when bad things happen in the world. Give them a resilient confidence in you as their great Savior and Lord. May their peaceful confidence in you cause others to look to you as their hope as well. Cause them to live life with a loose grip on material things and a firm hold on you. Make them generous with their lives and resources, blessing others when it is in their power to do so. Create in them a desire and devotion to helping others in the now. Create in them an urgency to do good when they can. For your glory and their good, in Jesus' name, amen.

Write down any thoughts or ideas you may want to **Share**:

Day Seven

Father, open my eyes so that I might *see* you more clearly, *savor* you more fully, and *share* you more freely.

Circle or underline any key words or phrases you **See**:

Do not plan evil against your neighbor, who dwells trustingly beside you. Do not contend with a man for no reason, when he has done you no harm. Do not envy a man of violence and do not choose any of his ways, for the devious person is an abomination to the LORD, but the upright are in his confidence. The LORD's curse is on the house of the wicked, but he blesses the dwelling of the righteous. Toward the scorners he is scornful, but to the humble he gives favor. The wise will inherit honor, but fools get disgrace. (Proverbs 3:29-35)

Savor these truths in prayer:

> Father, all your ways are good and those who walk in your wisdom will inherit honor. I pray that _____ will walk humbly in your wisdom so they may know the sweetness of your favor and honor. Keep them from ever planning harm against others and help them to stop others from doing so as well. Make them peacemakers in their relationships. Give them eyes to see when they are becoming contentious and give them grace to turn quickly away from that path. Remind them that the devious are always at odds with you and will never receive your blessing, but those who walk uprightly will know the depth of your favor and goodness. In Jesus' name, amen.

Write down any thoughts or ideas you may want to **Share**:

Notes

Week Fourteen

Leverage Prayers

A leverage prayer is a Scripture passage that displays a prayer and effect framework. This definition may never find its way into Webster's or dictionary.com, but it provides us with clarity as we use Scripture to pray powerfully and effectively. Leverage prayers can be identified by transitional phrases like "so that," "that you may," and "so as to." These phrases create a bridge from the prayer to the benefits of praying it. Leverage prayers are gifts from God to help us understand what can happen when we pray for specific things. Use the See, Savor, Share process to make the most of these leverage prayers:

1. *See*: Identify the key components of the prayer and the benefits of the "so that" section in each prayer.
2. *Savor*: Make these prayers your own. Hover over key portions that God causes to resonate with you, and savor them in prayer for a season.
3. *Share*: Be intentional about sharing the greatness of God you are seeing and savoring in prayer with those God brings into your life, especially your grandchildren!

Day One

Father, open my eyes so that I might *see* you more clearly, *savor* you more fully, and *share* you more freely.

For this reason, because I have heard of your faith in the Lord Jesus and your love toward all the saints, I do not cease to give thanks for you, remembering you in my prayers, that the God of our Lord Jesus Christ, the Father of glory, may give you the Spirit of wisdom and of revelation in the knowledge of him, having the eyes of your hearts enlightened, **that you may** *know what is the hope to which he has called you, what are the riches of his glorious inheritance in the saints, and what is the immeasurable greatness of his power toward us who believe, according to the working of his great might that he worked in Christ when he raised him from the dead and seated him at his right hand in the heavenly places, far above all rule and authority and power and dominion, and above every name that is named, not only in this age but also in the one to come. And he put all things under his feet and gave him as head over all things to the church, which is his body, the fullness of him who fills all in all. (Ephesians 1:15-23)*

Prayer:

Benefits of the prayer:

Day Two

Father, open my eyes so that I might *see* you more clearly, *savor* you more fully, and *share* you more freely.

For this reason I bow my knees before the Father, from whom every family in heaven and on earth is named, that according to the riches of his glory he may grant you to be strengthened with power through his Spirit in your inner being, **so that Christ may** *dwell in your hearts through faith—that you, being rooted and grounded in love, may have strength to comprehend with all the saints what is the breadth and length and height and depth, and to know the love of Christ that surpasses knowledge, that you may be filled with all the fullness of God.* (Ephesians 3:14-19)

Prayer:

Benefits of the prayer:

Day Three

Father, open my eyes so that I might *see* you more clearly, *savor* you more fully, and *share* you more freely.

And it is my prayer that your love may abound more and more, with knowledge and all discernment, **so that you may** *approve what is excellent, and so be pure and blameless for the day of Christ, filled with the fruit of righteousness that comes through Jesus Christ, to the glory and praise of God. (Philippians 1:9-11)*

Prayer:

Benefits of the prayer:

Day Four

Father, open my eyes so that I might *see* you more clearly, *savor* you more fully, and *share* you more freely.

And so, from the day we heard, we have not ceased to pray for you, asking that you may be filled with the knowledge of his will in all spiritual wisdom and understanding, **so as to** *walk in a manner worthy of the Lord, fully pleasing to him, bearing fruit in every good work and increasing in the knowledge of God. May you be strengthened with all power, according to his glorious might, for all endurance and patience with joy, giving thanks to the Father, who has qualified you to share in the inheritance of the saints in light. (Colossians 1:9-12)*

Prayer:

Benefits of the prayer:

Day Five

Father, open my eyes so that I might *see* you more clearly, *savor* you more fully, and *share* you more freely.

*...and may the Lord make you increase and abound in love for one another and for all, as we do for you, **so that he may** establish your hearts blameless in holiness before our God and Father, at the coming of our Lord Jesus with all his saints. (1 Thessalonians 3:12-13)*

Prayer:

Benefits of the prayer:

Day Six

Father, open my eyes so that I might *see* you more clearly, *savor* you more fully, and *share* you more freely.

To this end we always pray for you, that our God may make you worthy of his calling and may fulfill every resolve for good and every work of faith by his power, **so that the name of our Lord Jesus may** *be glorified in you, and you in him, according to the grace of our God and the Lord Jesus Christ.* (2 Thessalonians 1:11-12)

Prayer:

Benefits of the prayer:

Day Seven

Father, open my eyes so that I might *see* you more clearly, *savor* you more fully, and *share* you more freely.

*Now may the God of peace who brought again from the dead our Lord Jesus, the great shepherd of the sheep, by the blood of the eternal covenant, equip you with everything good **that you may** do his will, working in us that which is pleasing to his sight, through Jesus Christ, to whom be glory forever and ever. Amen. (Hebrews 13:20-21)*

Prayer:

Benefits of the prayer:

Notes

APPENDIX

Top summary results from our grandparent surveys

Let me state the obvious, we are not The Barna Group or Gallup or any other major polling or research group. However, as a generationally focused ministry that cares deeply about grandparents and their impact for generations to come, we decided to launch our own survey. We wanted to know some of the concerns and hopes of grandparents around the country, so we reached out to our friends and grandparent networks to help us get the word out about our survey. Through the process we were able to get a vast swath of responses to our grandparent survey, tapping into some of people's thoughts as Christian grandparents. I have distilled the most pertinent findings below, focusing on challenges and hopes.

The Top 3 Challenges for grandparents:

1. Distance from grandchildren
2. Limited time to spend with grandchildren
3. Not having enough energy to keep up with them/health challenges

The Top 3 Hopes and Desires grandparents have for their grandchildren!

1. They would know and love Jesus

2. They would continue to grow in their faith
3. Their health and safety

Of course these are not all of the hopes, desires and challenges that Grandparents have but they are the ones that rose to the top in our surveys and these results are not surprising. They probably reflect some of your own core hopes, desires and challenges as well. For me personally, I am delighted that the top two hopes and desires focus on grandchildren trusting and treasuring Christ. It is this relationship with Christ that will make all the difference concerning how our grandchildren flourish in this life and most certainly for eternity. The challenges were a different story. When looking over the responses to the surveys you could feel the heartache that grandparents are feeling because of distance, time and physical limitations. Thankfully there is technology that goes a long way in helping to bridge the chasm of not being there in person as much as they would like.

The hopes, desires and challenges from our survey point to the importance of this Prayer Guide. Through prayer we can ask the Lord from anywhere in the world to do for our grandchildren what only he can do. Through prayer we are not limited by distance, time or our own physical abilities. Prayer is God's supernatural way of allowing us to supersede our limitations to influence our grandchildren for his glory and their good. This is why this book is so important. You, as a grandparent can make a difference in your grandchildren's lives in spite of your limitations when you pray for them.

Pete Austin III Book of the Bible Prayer Approach

During my grandparent interview with Pete and Linda Austin, Pete shared one of his strategies for praying for his family. Each year he chooses one book of the Bible and after reading it through a number of times, he finds seven verses from that book to pray each day of the week for his family members. He uses this rhythm of biblical prayers as one of the ways he prays for each family member throughout the year. He also finds a verse for the year, savors it, letting it sink into and influence his life. He has graciously shared some of the past years of his approach with me and now I'm offering them to you. Feel free to adopt this approach to invigorate your prayers for your family. I know of one person who was inspired to use this approach for shorter time frames like, quarterly or monthly. Thank you, Pete for inspiring us with this approach for praying scripture.

Below are examples of Pete's approach. The first two examples are representative of the page that Pete creates for himself. I didn't want you to miss out on the goodness that flows from Pete's biblical focus, so I included a few more years in a condensed form. Of course, this is meant to inspire you. Enjoy!

Prayer for our family – from Hebrews (The "Let us" verses)

List family members names here:

SUNDAY – Let us then with confidence draw near to the throne of grace, that we may receive mercy and find grace to help in time of need. 4:16

MONDAY – Since we have a great priest over the house of God, let us draw near with a true heart in full assurance of faith, with our hearts sprinkled clean from an evil conscience and our bodies washed with pure water. 10:21-22

TUESDAY – Let us hold fast the confession of our hope without wavering, for he who promised is faithful. 10:23

WEDNESDAY – Let us consider how to stir up one another to love and good works. 10:24

THURSDAY – Therefore, since we are surrounded by so great a cloud of witnesses, let us also lay aside every weight, and sin which clings so closely, and let us run with endurance the race that is set before us, looking to Jesus. 12:1-2a

FRIDAY – Therefore let us be grateful for receiving a kingdom that cannot be shaken, and thus let us offer to God acceptable worship, with reverence and awe, for our God is a consuming fire. 12:28-29

SATURDAY – Through him then let us continually offer up a sacrifice of praise to God, that is, the fruit of lips that acknowledge his name. 13:15

MY VERSE FOR THE YEAR – Know this, my beloved brothers: let every person be quick to hear, slow to speak, slow to anger. James 1:19

Prayer for our family – adapted from John 17 (Jesus' High Priestly prayer)

List family members names here:

SUNDAY – May we know You the only true God, and Jesus Christ whom You have sent (v3), and may we keep Your word (v6).

MONDAY – May we receive Your words and come to know in truth that Jesus came from You, Father; may we believe that You sent the Son (v8); and may the Son be glorified in us (v10).

TUESDAY – Holy Father, keep us in Your name, which You have given to the Son, that we may be one, even as You and the Son are one (v11), and may we have Christ's joy fulfilled in ourselves (v13).

WEDNESDAY – As Jesus prayed, I do not ask that You take us out of the world, but that You keep us from the evil one (v15), and sanctify us in the truth; Your word is truth (v17). Again, may we be sanctified in truth (v19).

THURSDAY – May we all be one, just as You, Father, are in the Son, and the Son in You (v21). The Son in us and You in the Son, that we may become perfectly one, so that the world may know that You, Father, sent the Son and loved us even as You loved the Son (v23).

FRIDAY – May we also, whom You, Father, have given to the Son, be with the Son where He is, to see His glory that You have given Him because You loved Him before the foundation of the world (v24).

SATURDAY – Blessed Lord Jesus Christ, only Son of the Father, our Savior, King, and Friend, please continue to make known to us Your name, that the love with which the Father loved You may be in us, and You in us (v26).

MY VERSE FOR THE YEAR – Micah 6:8 – What does the Lord require of you but to do justice, and to love kindness, and to walk humbly with your God?

Additional Years Condensed

Prayer for our family – from 1 Peter:

Sunday – 1:15-16; Monday – 2:2; Tuesday – 2:11; Wednesday – 2:15; Thursday – 3:15; Friday – 4:13; Saturday – 5:6-7
My verse for 2017 – Philippians 2:3-4

Prayer for our family – from 2 Thessalonians:

Sunday – 1:2; Monday – 1:3; Tuesday – 1:11-12; Wednesday – 2:16-17; Thursday – 3:1-2; Friday – 3:3,5; Saturday – 3:16;
My verse for 2016 – (Psalm 139:23-24)!

Prayer for our family – from Colossians

Sunday – 1:10; Monday – 2:2-3; Tuesday – 2:6-7; Wednesday – 2:8; Thursday – 3:1-2; Friday – 3:12-13; Saturday – 3:23-24;
My verse for the year – Colossians 1:10

Prayer for our family – from 1 Thessalonians:

Sunday – 3:12-13; Monday – 4:3,4; Tuesday – 4:11,12; Wednesday - 5:14,15; Thursday - 5:16,18; Friday – 5:19-22; Saturday – 5:23-24.
My verse for the year – Romans 8:38-39

Prayer for our family – from Ephesians:

Sunday – 1:17-19a; Monday – 3:16-17a; Tuesday – 3:17b-19; Wednesday – 4:1b-2; Thursday – 4:29; Friday – 5:10-11; Saturday – 6:11
My verse for the year– Psalm 19:14

Prayer for our family – from 1 Corinthians

Sunday – 1:4; Monday – 2:5; Tuesday – 10:12-13; Wednesday – 10:31; Thursday – 13:4-5 & 14:1; Friday – from 14:20; Saturday – 15:58
My verse for the year – 1 Corinthians 13:4 – Love is patient and kind.

Prayer for our family – from Philippians:

Sunday – 1:3,8,9; Monday – 2:3-4; Tuesday – 3:8; Wednesday – 3:13-14; Thursday – 4:4,6; Friday – 4:8; Saturday – 4:19
My verse for the year – Philippians 4:6

Grandaddy Moose Nanny Gammy
Gramma Pappy
Nana Tank Gigi Granna Gram Hoss
Gampa Jan Grammy Granny
Chief Grandad Grandma Mimi Dandy
Bapa Pop Tink
Memaw Mumzie
Pap Opa Paps
Boppa Nannaw Mini
Mammaw Bibi Baba
Bobby
Sug Tattaw Grandmommy
Bella Bumpa Grandpa Pops Nina
Dot Gran Papa Daddy
Nini Memah Yiayia
Gramps Mama Gamma Pawpaw Poppy

PRAY for ME™ CAMPAIGN

Linking the Generations through Prayer

There is no doubt that every grandchild in every church needs multiple adult believers in their corner who are cheering them on in faith and life.

The Pray for Me Campaign is a simple way of creating these relationships in a natural and winsome way through the catalyst of prayer.

Here is how it works:

Students and families — **INVITE** → **Believers from multiple** — **GENERATIONS** → **To pray for 1 year through** — **THE PRAYER GUIDE**

As a grandparent you can play a decisive role in helping the young people in your church be relationally connected with every generation by helping your church launch the Pray for Me Campaign.

Find out more at: www.prayformecampaign.com

Become a Movement Champion!

Movement Champions are people who have seen and savored the benefits of the Pray for Me Campaign and now they want to share it with the world. Becoming a Movement Champion is a simple commitment with a big impact and involves three simple steps:

1. **Pray**: A Movement Champion prays for the advancement of the Pray for Me Campaign.

2. **Share**: A Movement Champion spreads the word about the Pray for Me Campaign.

3. **Give**: A Movement Champion gives financially to advance the Pray for Me Campaign.

Become a Movement Champion today at:
www.prayformecampaign.com/give

PRAY FOR ME
RESOURCES

ADULTS PRAYING FOR STUDENTS
Praying for middle and high school students

ADULTS PRAYING FOR CHILDREN
Praying for children fifth
grade and below.

STUDENT PRAYER GUIDE
Students praying for
their peers.

check out our other books and resources at
WWW.PRAYFORMECAMPAIGN.COM

Additional Resources

The Legacy Coalition

The Legacy Coalition is the world's largest source for grandparenting resources. They are all about helping grandparents have greater spiritual impact on their families. They know that Christian grandparents have an important spiritual role to play and they are seeking to help them become more intentional in that role. Visit them at leacycoalition.com.

Resilient by Valerie Bell

What we do today can shape the future of how young people follow Christ tomorrow and generations to come. The authors of *Resilient* have masterfully given us a vision of how we can help each emerging generation become resilient disciples who follow Christ for a lifetime. Read this resource and be infused with hope for the fearless future of the Church.

Faith for Exiles by David Kinnaman and Mark Matlock

It is easy to become discouraged by all that's going wrong when it comes to Christianity and the emerging generation. Yet, in *Faith for Exiles*, the authors unveil signs of hope that are springing up all around. Their research reveals five practices that contribute to resilient faith, of which meaningful intergenerational relationships are a core component.